MOM
RAGE

MOM RAGE

THE EVERYDAY CRISIS OF MODERN MOTHERHOOD

MINNA DUBIN

SEAL PRESS

New York

Seal Press
Hachette Book Group
1290 Avenue of the Americas, New York, NY 10104
www.sealpress.com
@sealpress

Printed in the United States of America

First Edition: September 2023

Published by Seal Press, an imprint of Hachette Book Group, Inc. The Seal Press name
and logo is a trademark of the Hachette Book Group.

The Hachette Speakers Bureau provides a wide range of authors for speaking events. To
find out more, go to www.hachettespeakersbureau.com or call (866) 376-6591.

Seal Press books may be purchased in bulk for business, educational, or promotional use.
For information, please contact your local bookseller or Hachette Book Group Special
Markets Department at special.markets@hbgusa.com.

The publisher is not responsible for websites (or their content) that are not owned by the
publisher.

Print book interior design by Amy Quinn.

Library of Congress Cataloging-in-Publication Data

Names: Dubin, Minna, author.
Title: Mom rage : the everyday crisis of modern motherhood / Minna Dubin.
Description: First edition. | New York, NY : Seal Press, [2023] | Includes bibliographical
  references and index.
Identifiers: LCCN 2022059121 | ISBN 9781541601307 (hardcover) | ISBN
  9781541601314 (ebook)
Subjects: LCSH: Motherhood—Social aspects. | Mothers—Social conditions. |
  Mothers—Conduct of life. | Mothers—Psychology.
Classification: LCC HQ759 .D787 2023 | DDC 306.874/3—dc23/eng/20230327
LC record available at https://lccn.loc.gov/2

ISBNs: 9781541601307 (hardcover), 9781541601314 (ebook)

LSC-C

Printing 1, 2023

For the mamas doing the damn thing—
in spite of their rage and because of it

Women have often felt insane when cleaving to the truth of our experience. Our future depends on the sanity of each of us, and we have a profound stake, beyond the personal, in the project of describing our reality as candidly and fully as we can to each other.

—Adrienne Rich, *Women and Honor: Some Notes on Lying*

Silence and shame are contagious; so are courage and speech. Even now, when women begin to speak of their experience, others step forward to bolster the earlier speaker and to share their own experience. A brick is knocked loose, another one; a dam breaks, the waters rush forth.

—Rebecca Solnit, *The Mother of All Questions*

CONTENTS

PROLOGUE

Mom rage is an anger so hot it is blinding. I was terrified when mine showed up, at first in intermittent blips, then every month, every week, until my rage was a constant low-grade buzzing beneath my skin. I consoled myself with excuses: *it's the four-month sleep regression, it's the hormonal shift from weaning.* But two years into motherhood, I was still slamming car doors, screaming at my partner outside Target, and working to keep my hands busy while the rage ripped through me so I wouldn't touch my son in a rough way. I had no excuses left.

Desperate to understand, I turned to our modern-day sage and fool—the Google search bar. A small balloon of hope inflated as I typed "mother rage" and pressed *Enter,* hoping the results would tell me I wasn't alone and save me from my fear that I was just a "moody bitch" (the hateful words used to denigrate angry women, which we internalize, then whisper back to ourselves).

All hail the internet! Amidst its dark chaos, I found Anne Lamott's 1998 essay "Mother Rage: Theory and Practice." I sat on my couch, reading her words and laughing out loud between sobs:

> At other people's homes, my child does not suck the energy and air out of the room. He does not do the same

annoying thing over and over and over until his friends'
parents need to ask him through clenched teeth to stop
doing this. But at our house, he—*comment se dit?*—fucks
with me. He can provoke me into a state of something
similar to road rage.

Lamott recounts ripped-off doll heads and doors slammed so
hard things fall off walls. Goose bumps of recognition rolled up
and down my arms as I read. I had found it! Levity! A comrade!
Proof I was perhaps not a mommy monster after all! Bolstered by
Lamott's bravery, I gave myself permission to say the unsayable. I
submitted an essay to the *New York Times*, which they ran under
the headline "The Rage Mothers Don't Talk About."

The rage lives in my hands, rolls down my fingers clench-
ing to fists. I want to hurt someone. I am tears and fury
and violence. I want to scream and rip open pillows, toss
chairs and punch walls. I want to see my destruction—
feathers floating, overturned furniture, ragged holes in
drywall.
    When I get mad like this around my three-year-old
son, I have to say to myself, like a mantra, "Don't touch
him, don't touch him, don't touch him." Touching him
with this rage coursing through me only ends in my
shame, and my son's shock, and what else I do not know;
only time will reveal that. I have never hit him, but the
line between "hitting" and "not hitting" is porous. In this
"not hitting" gray area there are soft arms squeezed too
tight, a red superhero cape (Velcro-clasped around his
neck) forcefully yanked off, a child picked up and thrown
into his crib. For me it is better not to touch at all. Only
a few years ago, I remember judging a mother on the bus

for smacking her child. Now I have only empathy for her. Mother rage can change you, providing access to parts of yourself you didn't even know you had.

Hundreds of mothers from around the world wrote to me in response. Each of their messages was more or less identical: "I thought I was the worst mother in the world. I am so ashamed."

Shame doesn't like its baggage aired in public. Talking about it loosens its grip, freeing us to move toward something else. With each mother's confession, I felt my own shame unhook. I began to move into a place of questioning.

What if the conclusion I, and the moms who were writing to me, had come to—that each of us must be "the worst mother in the world"—was untrue? What if we were normal mothers reacting to unjust circumstances? What if mom rage were a widespread, culturally created phenomenon, and not just a personal problem?

These questions spurred an in-depth investigation into mom rage that became this book. For three years, I spoke to moms across the country—and around the world—about their rage. This book draws on these mothers' experiences, along with my own decade-long mom rage journey, combined with research and cultural critique, to uncover what mom rage is, why we have it, and what we can do about it.

In the first few chapters, I explore the broader societal landscape that sets up today's mothers for despair and fury. The focus of the middle of the book narrows to the individual and shows how, in addition to being a legitimate reaction to the cultural oppression of mothers, mom rage is also a nuanced physiological and psychological experience. Mom rage presents as a singular explosion but in fact there is activity happening in our bodies and psyches long before and long after the moment of expressed fury.

I break this activity down into phases that make up what I call the "Mom Rage Cycle." Next, I share strategies to better understand our rage, identify personal rage triggers, and make allies of our partners in the effort to alleviate our rage. The final chapters look at how mothers can be better cared for by societal systems and through alternative family structures and community support networks.

I wrote this book to help you with your mom rage *today*, and I wrote it to spur systemic change in the hope that future generations of mothers won't even know what mom rage is. But if they do, they'll at least be able to speak about it without shame.

Most of the moms I interviewed did not want to use their real names for this book. I understand their fear. I, too, am afraid to put my rage on record. The confines of "appropriate" or "good" motherhood—which come from white, wealthy, patriarchal ideas of mothering—are so strict that mom rage can feel both unforgivable and unspeakable. But every time I speak or write about it, other mothers rescue me with their own vulnerability. Mothers who seem to have it all together reach out to me privately and say, "Me too." Some of them haven't raged in a decade but have not been able to let their shame go.

Talking about mom rage yanks it down from the scary place it looms in our minds, and enables us to engage with the tenderness that lives inside it. Speaking mom rage out loud is a way of staking a claim for oneself. *I am worthy of forgiveness. I am worthy of care. My experience matters.* Oppression strives to strip away people's power by silencing their voices and trivializing their experiences. In *The Mother of All Questions*, Rebecca Solnit writes, "Liberation is always in part a storytelling process: breaking stories, breaking silences, making new stories. A free person tells her own story. A valued person lives in a society in which her story has a place."

This book places mothers' voices at its center. Their tales of maternal anger resist the societal mandate that mothers' purpose in life is to provide nurture at all costs, even to our own detriment, even if it means erasing ourselves. Each story that drags mom rage out of its shame corner into the light is an assertion of self. I hope *Mom Rage* provides mothers respite from the shame, the loneliness, and the mean voices—both internal and external. And once that shame has been released, I hope it moves us all toward creating a more equitable and joyful motherhood, where we are adequately cared for, and our stories are honored for the wisdom they possess.

———

When I began my investigation into maternal anger, I had a lot of basic questions about what mom rage was—and what it wasn't. The answers I uncovered impacted the choices I made in writing this book, and I'm presenting them here as a kind of "Mom Rage 101."

WHO EXPERIENCES MOM RAGE?

The short answer is any mom can have mom rage, though cultural factors like race and class matter in a variety of ways, which I'll delve into in the book. I interviewed and surveyed fifty mothers from a range of backgrounds who identify as having mom rage. I talked to moms who identify as white, Caribbean Canadian, Black, Afro Latina, multiracial, Latinx, and mestiza. The Asian mothers I interviewed have a wide range of identities, including Taiwanese American, Taiwanese Canadian, Indian, Cambodian, Singaporean Chinese Canadian, South Asian, Chinese American, and Kalmyk Mongol American.

I discovered through my interviews with mothers who are Muslim, Christian, Jewish, agnostic, Buddhist, and Hindu that mom rage does not discriminate based on how religious one is or the religion one practices. The raging mothers I talked to are married or otherwise partnered, single, or divorced. The moms and their partners are straight, queer, and questioning. The gender identities of the mothers, their partners, and their children are cisgender, genderqueer, nonbinary, transgender, and questioning.

The interviewees fall into economic brackets across the spectrum. Some struggle with putting food on the table and finding free summer camp options. Others enjoy luxuries like owning their own home and being able to pay for therapy out of pocket. Most work full- or part-time paid jobs. I interviewed an executive director of an NGO, an Ayurveda practitioner who makes and sells dosas at a local market, a yoga teacher, a health policy researcher, a diversity manager, a PhD student, and a nighttime caregiver. I also talked to stay-at-home moms, most of whom have a side hustle. Two have multilevel marketing jobs. One sells nail polish.

Some of the moms send their kids to school (public and private) and others homeschool. They live all over the United States, from Moonachie, New Jersey, to Calabasas, California, to Kurtistown, Hawaii. Because mom rage affects parents across the globe, I cast a wide net and interviewed moms experiencing rage from Canada, South Africa, Israel, the Netherlands, the United Kingdom, New Zealand, Australia, Germany, and Ireland.

The moms in this book are bio moms, foster moms, adoptive moms, stepmoms, and moms who underwent years of fertility treatments. The mothers I talked to have anywhere from one to seven children, from newborn to adult. Rage crept up on some of them during pregnancy. For others, it took years of parenting—and sometimes an additional child—before they felt that spark of anger grow bright. Some of the mothers I spoke with were funny and warm, their words tumbling out faster than my fingers could fly across the keyboard. Others were more guarded, and I could feel the weight of the shame between us. For many of the moms, our interview was the first time they'd been asked about their rage. There were a lot of tears.

Not every story made it into the book. I tried to use a sampling that felt representative of the varied experiences. All the moms' names and some identifying details have been changed.

WHY USE THE GENDERED LANGUAGE OF *MOTHER*?

For me, *mother* is a spacious word with room for all its children. As a verb, I use *to mother* to mean to nurture, which is something anyone can do regardless of sex or gender. Mother connotes the depth of the caregiving, its all-encompassing nature. Anyone who performs that labor is included when I talk about mothers in this book, including those of you who use other monikers that better fit your gender identity, including but not limited to Baba, Dama, Moppa, and Pama.

I intentionally use gender inclusive language where I can. When I'm talking about a hypothetical person at a prenatal appointment, I might use *pregnant person*. When I'm talking about someone in labor, I might use *birthing person*. These phrases are meant to include trans and nonbinary people who are birthing and parenting. Sometimes I call someone a mother before the baby is out of their body. This is also intentional. For some people, the identity transformation of becoming a mother begins long before the baby ever makes a sound. Some people whose babies are stillborn also identify as mothers. There are numerous ways to be a mother.

I made the choice to use she/her pronouns when speaking about a hypothetical mother—or mothers in general—because mom rage is not divorced from gender. It didn't make sense to use an all-inclusive term like *parent rage*, because "dad rage" is not on the same playing field as mom rage. (I'll dive into exactly why later in this book.) I use she/her pronouns to honor the massive role sexism, misogyny, and patriarchy play in the oppression of mothers, which leads to anger. These power dynamics, in addition to the gendered expectations of mothers, affect all mothering people regardless of their gender identity.

So, for my fellow queers and my nonbinary and trans readers: know that while I am centering *mother* and using she/her pronouns, I am talking to you too.

IS MOM RAGE CONNECTED TO POSTPARTUM DEPRESSION?

The correlation between mom rage and postpartum mood and anxiety disorders (PMADs) is tricky, mostly because there isn't enough research on maternal anger. Anger can be a symptom of both postpartum depression and postpartum anxiety. Mothers can also experience rage without having a PMAD. Some of the moms I interviewed were diagnosed with a PMAD after birth. Others were not. Some thought they probably had one but were never diagnosed. Personally, I was never diagnosed with a PMAD. My mom rage erupted in earnest when I began weaning my first child, between nine and twelve months. By then, no one was screening me for a PMAD anymore. Was my rage just hormones? Is my rage an undiagnosed PMAD? Can we call it a PMAD if it's three years postpartum? What about eight years? Twelve? It's muddy territory.

In addition to not having enough established research to draw a definitive link between PMADs and mom rage, I also want to avoid pathologizing mom rage. Classifying it as a medical condition relieves society and fathers of the responsibility to take care of mothers and families. I see mom rage as an understandable reaction (albeit not good for anyone) to oppressive cultural circumstances.

IS MOM RAGE CHILD ABUSE?

The time I spent hunting down past and present instances of maternal anger turned up very little that wasn't salacious, like "The 25 Worst Moms in History." Spoiler alert!—they all murdered their children. In Americans' collective consciousness, angry moms are equated with murderers—or at least abusers—because there is no room in the claustrophobic box of Mother for anything other than self-sacrificing, gentle, and deferential.

Though the history of maternal rage remains elusive, female anger does not. And since most women in history were mothers, the two histories are intertwined. The culture's impulse to extinguish angry women can be traced back centuries. In their book *Witchcraft and Magic in Sixteenth- and Seventeenth-Century Europe*, scholars Geoffrey Scarre and John Callow write that witches were well known for their "quarrelsome and aggressive nature." The execution of hundreds of thousands of people for witchcraft from the fourteenth to seventeenth centuries in Europe, and then in America, may well have been a mass slaughter of angry women. By the 1800s, women suspected of rejecting their station in life weren't being hanged anymore; they were being committed for insanity instead. The culture's need to control and fix angry women continued as women who exhibited anger, anxiety, or virtually anything that was unpleasant to the men in their lives found themselves diagnosed with hysteria.

Given this history of diagnosing, blaming, punishing, and even destroying women for being angry, I want to be very careful not to get caught in the societal pull to conflate women's anger with harm.

Anything can be harmful when taken to the extreme: running, substance use, caregiving, anger. While mom rage is not the equivalent of abuse, it does hold the potential for such harm. Mothers who experience rage know this in their marrow. It is the skeleton shape of their shame. Rage is a natural reaction to the cultural disempowerment of mothers, but that doesn't free us of responsibility for how we express that anger. Abuse is an act that causes serious physical or emotional harm. It is never okay.

In this book, I talk about mom rage within a non-abuse framework. I urge all parents who feel out of control to seek support.

IS MOM RAGE SPECIFIC TO THE COVID-19 PANDEMIC?

Though I wrote this book during the heart of the pandemic, it is not centered on pandemic motherhood. I directly address the pandemic a few times, but even when I'm not explicitly mentioning its effect on mothers' lives, the pandemic lingers in the space between words. How could it not? Unable to go to our workspaces during the pandemic, my partner and I took turns using our bedroom as an office. For months, I sat cross-legged on our bed, laptop propped on a pillow on my lap. Eventually my aching body screamed, *Your thirties are over*, and I bought a tiny desk. I typed away at it, four feet from the closed door— a slight and intermittent barrier to the constancy of pandemic mothering. When I interviewed mothers, we were up against the ever-present clock of our children's needs, our own needs fading into the pandemic ether.

After mothering through a years-long pandemic, moms need to see their parenting realities reflected more than ever. Usually, when we picture motherhood, we see wobbly first steps taken on delicious, dimpled legs, kids saying the cutest things ever, soft arms and heads nuzzled against our necks. These images depict a *part* of motherhood, probably the most popular part, the part that makes couples say with a smile, "Let's have a baby!" The predominance of this googly-eyed, cooing narrative of motherhood obscures the harder parts that became even more extreme during the pandemic—the isolation, the ceaseless labor, the physical toll, the inequality that grows inside the parenting partnership, and the economic hit that impacts mothers' earning potential for the rest of their lives, to name a few. This book is a rebellion against the supremacy of the googly-eyed, cooing narrative, and the way it silences moms by erasing the harder parts of modern motherhood.

Mothers' anger has been stewing for years, decades, possibly centuries. The lack of information on the history of mom rage doesn't mean it isn't real or didn't exist before the pandemic. It means mothers' fury hasn't been deemed valuable by those with cultural power as a story worth investigating or preserving. With the way society punishes angry women and shames mothers who step out of their domestic box of caregiving, it has likely been undesirable—if not unsafe—for mothers to preserve their own mom rage history.

The pandemic did not make modern motherhood a recipe for mom rage. But when what little childcare infrastructure there was disintegrated in 2020, it was the final straw that stirred the collective rage of mothers into a battle cry that echoed across the globe. Mothers were finally ready to tell their rage stories—public scorn and shame be damned. This book is woven from those stories.

1 THE HOUSE OF MOM RAGE

> A house is never apolitical. It is conceived, con-
> structed, occupied, and policed by people with
> power, needs, and fears.
>
> —Carmen Maria Machado, *In the Dream House: A Memoir*

Mothers everywhere are raging.

After a stressful eight-hour workday, followed by an hourlong commute in traffic, a mother stands in the bathroom as her five-year-old daughter wriggles. She hops from foot to foot, sticking out her hip, turning the faucet on and off. Everything but brushing her teeth.

"Enough with the dancing," the mom sighs, a hint of irritation creeping into her voice. The daughter makes a show of standing on her tiptoes and doing a projectile spit. It misses the sink.

"Watch what you're doing!" The mother wipes up the spit with a square of toilet paper, thinking about the work she needs to catch up on once her daughter is in bed. The girl drops her toothbrush one, two, three times. She giggles at her own antics. The mom slams her palm against the wall.

"I'm serious. Stop!" She grabs the toothbrush out of her daughter's mouth.

"Why do we have to do this every day? Twice a day! Open!" The mother brushes her daughter's teeth quickly and roughly. The girl won't stop moving.

"You need to stand still or you're going to get hurt!" Five more seconds pass with the child's body gyrating before the inevitable happens—the daughter accidentally bonks the side of her head on the sink. She clutches her head and lets out a howl. The mom tosses the toothbrush into the sink, sits down on the toilet, puts her elbows on her knees, and presses the heels of her palms into her closed eyes. She knows if she speaks, she will blow the house down, and everyone in it.

Mom rage lives in the body. Fingers curl, cheeks burn, breathing quickens. Similar to road rage, mom rage bubbles up fast and hot. Mom rage is fury—mothers bursting with uncontrollable anger. Its release is often aural and physical: a rhythmic string of high-pitched curses; a booming trombone yell, so growly the mother's throat is sore the next morning; hands slapping out a sharp beat on her own stinging thighs; a bass drum foot pounding out each word—BRUSH (*stomp*) YOUR (*stomp*) TEETH (*stomp*) NOW (*stomp, stomp*)!!

As mothers, we know we are supposed to be nurturing, patient, gentle; never rageful. We try to hide our wrath, hold it in, keep it quiet. Sheila, mother to a three-year-old and seven-month-old in Brisbane, Australia, admitted to me in an email, "I often feel the rage and would sometimes just LOVE to stab a mattress into pieces with a very sharp knife." Sheila used to hide her rage by screaming underwater at her local public pool, but the pandemic robbed her of that covert release. When mom rage takes over, not physically hurting someone is an act of will. Joanna from Portugal told me, "I remember holding [my daughter] and biting down on her fluffy onesie to staunch something worse."

Those on the receiving end of mom rage are often our children, but not always. The vitriol can be directed at partners, pets, men in general, the system, or everyone around us. Mom rage can also turn inward, manifesting in self-harm: substance abuse, cutting, punching our thighs, slapping our own face, biting the insides of our lips, cheek, tongue—anything that can feel pain. Moms who rage are in pain, even if we don't know it.

That pain isn't caused by a child not wanting to brush her teeth, or any of the other daily irritations of parenting. Its foundations go much deeper. Mom rage stems from the overwhelming stress and impossible expectations of modern motherhood, combined with a debilitating lack of support from within the family structure and societal systems.

The sneaky thing about the causes of mom rage is that we can't *see* them. In their visual absence, all we see is an angry mom. On the surface, mom rage looks like simple cause and effect: a child drops a jar and it shatters, resulting in the mom yelling, hot-faced and wild. This explanation of mom rage is easy to comprehend—there was an action and then a reaction. Perhaps there are details that complicate the story and make the mother's strong reaction easier to empathize with. Maybe before this happened, the mother asked the child repeatedly not to play with the jar. Maybe the jar was the mother's only heirloom from her great-grandmother who escaped the Holocaust. Maybe the mother has a pending work deadline, and Grandma, who was supposed to babysit, just called out with a migraine.

If we imagine mom rage as a house, the cause-and-effect scenario is happening on the main floor—let's say, in the kitchen, since that is where so much of mothers' daily domestic work takes place. To fully understand mom rage, we have to leave the kitchen and descend to the basement to uncover what came before. By "before," I mean what happened the hour or day before the mother screamed at her child, but I also mean history—the mother's own personal history, and the larger cultural history that shapes the way we live, think, and breathe today. History, identity, social norms, power(lessness), and past trauma, in addition to current societal systems and attitudes, are all at work when a mom balls up her fists and roars at the people around her—often the people she loves most.

In the mom rage basement, we locate how a lack of partner support stems from cultural inequalities. Let's rewind the clock on the raging mother and her child who broke the jar. Maybe the mom is alone with the child every morning because the father leaves early to get to his job. Her husband makes less money than she does, but her boss allows her to work from home in the mornings to accommodate her motherly responsibilities. Her husband was not offered this same flexibility. But he also never asked for it because it didn't feel like part of his office's culture. None of the other men at his job work from home. Come to think of it, he's not even sure if any of them have kids. The mother's ability to partially work from home means that if their child gets sick and can't go to childcare, it doesn't matter if she has an important presentation at work. The responsibility to "figure it out" is hers. Her job flexibility and her husband's job inflexibility—which both seem innocuous but are the result of systemic inequality—have surreptitiously placed the primary responsibility for childcare squarely in her lap. Perhaps this is an irritation that grows a little more each day when her husband kisses her goodbye, while their child tantrums on the floor.

Maybe the night before the child dropped the jar, the mom asked her husband to find a higher shelf for his jar collection so their growing child wouldn't be able to reach it. Maybe her partner responded, "Relax." When we descend into the mom rage basement, we see that when the jar crashes the next day, the mother may seem angry at her child, but she is really hurt and angry with her husband for dismissing her concerns as unnecessary worrying. Underneath that, she is disappointed and mad at herself for allowing her partner's dismissal to silence her, for not trusting her own wisdom and moving the jars herself. In the mom rage basement, we witness the repetitive wounding of being a woman in a patriarchal society that constantly disregards and belittles us.

Mom rage's basement is packed floor to ceiling with dusty boxes, each one stuffed with evidence of the different ways mothers are disempowered in the home and by the culture at large, based on the identities we hold. If the mom in the house with the broken jar is Black, for example, she and her child are at much greater physical risk than a white mother and child. If someone outside hears the combination of shattering glass followed by screaming, they might call the police, which could lead to her being deemed an unfit mother by the state. Black children are taken from their mothers and put in out-of-home placements by child protective services at 2.2 times the rate of white children (2.9 times for Native American children). Black people are also approximately three times more likely to be killed by police than white people. These looming possibilities are fear- and fury-inducing, if not deeply traumatizing. The identities we each hold—fat, trans, immigrant, disabled, teenage—can incur daily social and systemic discrimination. This informs the way we experience motherhood in the world and adds more fury and trauma to the stockpile in our mom rage basements.

Structural inequalities, which cause pressure, stress, and anger, and can lead to poverty and health conditions, matter a great deal in the house of mom rage. Yet, it is a much cleaner narrative to keep mom rage in the kitchen: the child drops a jar; his mom yells. That narrative doesn't challenge the status quo. It doesn't shine a light on inequality or reveal a society that sets mothers up for defeat. It puts the blame squarely on the shoulders of the mother: *What kind of mother would lash out at her family that way?*

This question is asked both by the people who judge mothers struggling with mom rage and by the mothers themselves when they're in the post-rage moments of shame and guilt. Many mothers aren't aware of the growing piles in their mom rage basements. They think they are just furious at their kids or their partners, and that they need to get a grip on their anger. End of story. If mothers blame themselves and society blames them, too, then the problem of mom rage is seen as individual, absolving the society of any responsibility.

While history, identity, discrimination, and power dynamics are stacked in dusty boxes down in the basement, upstairs in the kitchen is a child who didn't heed his mother's warnings and made a potentially harmful mess. Anger is an option on the list of responses the mother can reach for in this moment. Other options are compassion, disappointment, worry, even humor. If only mom rage felt like a choice. Most mothers who rage aren't able to pause and take a moment to think, "What is the healthiest and most effective way to respond here?" Rage is faster than reason.

On her podcast, *Queenstown Life*, host Jane Guy from New Zealand describes her own mom rage as a little animal that lives inside her throat. She says the first time it appeared, "This beast came out of my throat from nowhere and I was like, '*Who was that?*' And then I got really scared because I didn't know where it was going to come from or at what point." She remembers a time when her mom rage came knocking at two o'clock in the morning. "My child had woken up for the three thousandth time. I remember going to my husband, 'I'LL DO IT!!' And he went,

'Whoa!' like, '*Who is that?*' And I just thought, '*There it is!*' I have no control over it."

Jane's feeling of having no control over "the beast in her throat" raises an important point about the relationship between anger and rage. Rage has a reputation for being angrier than anger—louder, more intense, more prolonged. While this may be true in some circumstances, the difference between anger and rage isn't simply one of degree. It's that the person experiencing rage feels out of control. Rage might feel, as in Jane's example, like someone or something has invaded or taken over. Another mom described her experience of mom rage as "an out of body experience, where it's almost like I split into two. One part of me is like, 'Oh, this is not good. I want to try and stop it.' But the majority of me is like, 'Nope, there's no stopping this.'" The rager is not making a conscious decision to begin yelling. It is as if the rage is happening *to* her.

Lack of control is a quintessential component of both the rage itself and the circumstances that set mothers up for it. Today's mothers are essentially stirring a commercial kitchen's worth of pots all at once, knowing that if we were to stop stirring even one, our lives might crumble down on top of us. On an ordinary day, a mother's mind might flit between seven different pots: (1) her children playing/fighting in the living room; (2) the beans bubbling (in an actual pot!) on the kitchen stove; (3) the plumber on her knees in the bathroom fixing the family's only toilet; (4) the dryer on its second delicate cycle to fully dry the pee pad for her eight-year-old's mattress; (5) the special education teacher at her son's school who didn't answer any of the mom's questions in her email, which makes her wonder if her kid is getting competent care and services; (6) her phone alerting her that it is her night on the meal train to bring lasagna to the neighbor friend who just had a baby; and (7) the clock over the bookshelf, which indicates the exact minute her wife will walk in the door and take over some of the pot-stirring, so she can snag the last few hours of the day for her freelance work.

Mothers are holding so much.

What is the likely outcome of adding an eighth pot for the mother to stir? The extra stressor that throws the mom into a rage might be the latest round of nightly gunshots outside her window. Or the weekly puzzle she must solve of needing to be in two places at once. Or her wife expecting her to attend the parent-teacher conference by herself—and then during the recap asking, "Why didn't you ask the teacher about X or Y?" The mother doesn't know, because she didn't think of those questions. Her wife seems annoyed, which feels righteously unfair because she is stirring a hundred pots! And—*boom*—she is levitating with rage.

Though mom rage can look like "boom" and feel like "boom," and sometimes even sound like "boom," it's actually more like a long, drawn out, silent "boooooooooooooooom" that is completely imperceptible to most ragers until the eventual explosion. Before a mom reaches rage, irritation and stress have been slowly building inside of her, possibly for hours, days, or even weeks. She may not be aware that, in addition to all the other invisible labor she's doing as a mother, she has been hard at work *not* raging for the entire time span her irritation has been rising into wrath. Mom rage is much more nuanced than "furious" or "not furious."

Most of the mothers I interviewed rage out loud, myself included. Our rage shows up as yelling, loud clapping, doors slamming. But just because a mother isn't yelling doesn't mean she isn't raging. For some moms, like Cheryl, their rage turns inward.

Cheryl, a forty-year-old, Black, middle-class civil rights lawyer in Rockville, Maryland, begins her day like most parents—stirring multiple pots. Cheryl said parenting her seven-year-old son is challenging from the moment the family wakes up. First, he doesn't want to put his clothes on, then he refuses every breakfast option Cheryl offers. "He doesn't want any of them. When I was a kid, I ate free lunch and free breakfast at school. We didn't have food."

Then comes the biggest pot to stir—getting her son to take his ADHD medicine. Cheryl and her husband have tried all the things: pouring the medicine from larger pill capsules into smaller ones, putting the medicine into pudding, making it into candy. "He fights us. He fights us. He fights us. That's how my day starts."

Cheryl described one day when her son was doing virtual school from home during the COVID-19 pandemic. He was frustrated because he didn't know what he was supposed to be doing. Cheryl suggested they ask the teacher, but her son's anxiety made him not want to ask. Instead, he began breaking pencils, one after the other, from a fresh box Cheryl had just bought him. She could feel her rage rising. "I wanted to shake him." Instead, Cheryl thought, "I can't put my hands on this child, because if I hold him, I'm going to squeeze really hard on purpose, because he's pissing me off." Cheryl walked herself back into her office, and let her son break every single pencil. "Now we just use half pencils. What am I going to do? I'm not buying any more pencils!"

In the mom rage kitchen, Cheryl's son did an action (he broke the pencils), and Cheryl had a reaction (she became enraged). But if we go into Cheryl's mom rage basement, we discover her personal history informing her present. Cheryl grew up in a home with a father who did not resist the urge to squeeze. "I remember one time he grabbed my hand and squeezed it really, really hard. I thought he was gonna break my hand. He didn't, but I could tell that he wanted to."

Her abusive home environment made it unsafe for Cheryl to express her anger growing up. "[As a teenager,] I would play

games on my phone so that I could turn off and numb myself."
Now, as a mother struggling with rage, Cheryl continues to hold
her anger inside. Trauma history is one of the boxes stacked in the
mom rage basement.

Mom rage began for Cheryl when her son was a newborn. "I
was sleep deprived and pissed at my husband. I don't know why;
he could've been breathing wrong. And the baby was screaming, and I felt like no one was doing anything." When her son
got older, before the ADHD medicine, Cheryl described him as
"a frickin' hurricane," who would "wake up and run." Cheryl
would get so exhausted and overwhelmed by her son's constant
motion and what seemed like his inability to listen, that sometimes she'd scream, throw, or break things. But more commonly,
she'd find a way to remove herself (either physically or mentally)
from the situation and the rage. She would often go into her bedroom, close the door, and pretend she was asleep. Other times
she'd drink wine and watch TV. "I never used to drink. But [after
becoming a mom] I started drinking more."

Sometimes staying in the house was too much. Cheryl remembered being so pissed off at her husband and her son and their
"moods" that one time she left without a word. Driving around,
she thought to herself, "I can't handle this. I need something to
take away this pain, this frustration. I don't want to feel it." She
ended up stocking up on booze at a liquor store. Then she drove
around vaping tobacco and listening to podcasts. She did not
drink while driving, she assures me. She did, however, drink that
liquor later.

Escaping our circumstances and our pain is one way mothers
try to get away from our rage. First we vanish our bodies (hide in
the bedroom, leave the house), then we flatten our minds (check
out with screen time, drink, or use drugs). The cultural messaging around drinking mothers—"mommy wine time"—makes

it less likely we'll ask ourselves if we're numbing our rage and more likely we'll see the escape it offers as a reward: "I deserve this glass of wine! It's been a long day!" Whether or not you think moms *deserve* a glass of sauvignon blanc, alcohol is not a substitute for the missing social infrastructure moms *need*, like universal preschool and specialized support for parents with neurodivergent children.

In *HuffPost*, writer and mother Amanda Montei writes that, during the pandemic, drinking offered moms "a *physiological* break: Drunkenness was a way some bodies could leave the house when they had no other exit." I'd argue that it offers this possibility for all mothers who feel suffocated by the perpetual labor of mom life, pandemic or not. Montei describes drinking as a way of "disappearing herself."

Wanting to disappear oneself is a self-harm response to pain, and a way to internalize the rage. Cheryl stops herself from unleashing her anger on her family by unleashing it on herself. In addition to drinking, her self-harm manifests as cutting, bingeing and purging, biting her nails to the quick, and pulling at her hair. "I pull it out and pull it out, and then at a certain point I have a bald spot and I'm like, 'Okay, let me just pluck my eyebrows,' but then I'll end up with no eyebrows."

Like mom rage, self-harm is a spectrum and can present in varying degrees of severity. I have also turned to alcohol and overeating to numb or harm myself when I'm struggling with mom rage. More than once, in the post-rage throes of guilt and shame, I have stared at my tear-streaked face in the mirror and slapped my cheeks as hard as I could. Whether a mother is self-harming to punish herself for raging or to try to stop the rage feelings in the first place, self-harm is a way mothers turn their fury onto themselves.

So what causes Cheryl to direct her rage inward?

Cheryl pointed to what she calls "intergenerational rage," stacked up in her mom rage basement—trauma passed down from her mother, and her mother's mother. I asked Cheryl what makes her think her grandmother had rage. "She's a Black woman! And a single mother. When I look at my grandmother's eyes in pictures, I see so much pain. I'm like, 'Damn, I feel that too.'" Cheryl described her own mom, who was also abused by Cheryl's father, as quiet. "She tried to just fade into the background. She disappeared. I realize that's what I'm becoming. I was able to create a different lifestyle in the sense that we're not in poverty anymore, but the emotional poverty is still with me."

Cheryl was struggling not just with internalizing her rage, but with being able to recognize what she's feeling in the first place. She was afraid her son may inherit this from her. Stopping the cycle of intergenerational rage and emotional poverty is what recently motivated Cheryl to get herself into therapy. "I've suffered for forty years with PTSD, and I'm only now thinking maybe I should deal with it."

It is not unique or surprising that Cheryl is only now considering getting into therapy. Society dictates that mothers put their families' needs first. Otherwise, we are labeled selfish moms. As a society, we shun and punish mothers who are deemed "selfish" or "mentally ill," even if that selfishness keeps the mother sane and healthy, and even if that psychiatric diagnosis is what enables the mother to get the treatment she needs to get well.

Cheryl suspected that feelings of unworthiness are at the heart of her internalized rage. "It's hard for me to love myself." She has an easier time accessing the love she feels for her son. "I always think to myself, 'He's infuriating, but don't you love him more than anything in the world?' And I'm like, 'Yeah! I do!' And I think, 'As annoying as he is, isn't he the most precious thing in the world?' And I'm like, 'Yeah! He is!' You know what? Maybe I can be precious too."

Maybe I can be precious too.

My body tingles with recognition. Far into my own mom rage journey, I, too, will discover that my feelings of unworthiness are tangled up with my rage. But I'm getting ahead of myself. Let me start at the beginning. My own mom rage showed up minimally during my son Ollie's first year. It didn't take hold and scare me until he was two.

On an ordinary day walking home from preschool, I pressed Ollie's velvety palm into mine as we stepped off the curb onto the crosswalk of a busy street with no light or stop sign. The oncoming cars idled. I felt proud as the drivers—happy captives, I imagined—watched my beautiful boy bounce across the street with me. He had loopy, light brown curls atop a sturdy body, and a smile that ignited joy.

Partway across the street, I felt a heavy tug on my arm. I looked down to see that Ollie had gone "boneless." He'd lifted his feet from the ground and made his body go limp. If I let go of his hand, tightly clasped in mine, he would crumple to the ground in the middle of the street. He smiled up at me as he hung in the air.

"Stop, Ollie! You have to walk!" I said in a high, panicky voice. He remained limp. A man leaned his head out of his car and said loudly, "Make his ass get up!" I felt offended that a total stranger was telling me what to do, but he was right—I had to get my baby out of the street!

Ollie was heavy, but I could still lift him if I had to. I scooped him up and walked a few more feet, plopping him down on the median in the middle of the street, so the waiting cars could go by. Once they passed, I carried Ollie back across the street to the sidewalk where we began. I felt indignant.

"You cannot do that, Ollie! No games in the street or I'll give you a time out! We are going to try again. Are you gonna walk now?" He looked at me and shook his head no with a small smile.

"Then you are gonna sit here until you're ready!" I exclaimed and pushed down on his shoulders. Down went Ollie's butt onto the ground. Maybe his balance was off. Maybe I pushed too hard. His upper body followed, and the back of his head hit the sidewalk behind him with a *thunk*. My hands flew to my mouth. I kneeled down and pulled him up toward me.

"Are you okay?" I asked, horrified. He looked at me bewildered. I imagined the question, *Did you hurt me, Mama?* flit across his eyes. Had I? I pulled his head to my chest.

"It's okay, you're okay," I chanted as I rocked him back and forth. Safe in my arms, Ollie began to wail. A woman walked by, and her pointed look told me she'd seen everything and did not approve. *Fuck you*, I thought and pressed my lips into Ollie's fine hair.

Eventually, his little head intact, Ollie calmed, and we managed to cross the street together with no more rage and no more boneless antics. Once we made it safely to the other side, Ollie jumped and twirl-spun the rest of the way home. I filled with relief as I watched my little boy spin, arms open to the world. Despite my moment of fear-panic-indignation-fury-aggression-guilt-shame, it seemed I had not destroyed my very best thing.

At the time of this incident, I'd never heard of mom rage, and I certainly hadn't descended into my mom rage basement. I was stuck in the kitchen with its one-to-one causality: my kid acted out; I lost my shit. I couldn't see anything beyond my inability to control myself.

Here's what was happening below the floorboards: that year, Ollie began hurting other kids at school. My partner, Paul, works full time, and I was making no money then, trying my darnedest to be a writer. This meant I did most of the preschool drop-offs and pickups, which I enjoyed until Ollie began being physically aggressive with other children. Suddenly pickups became the time when the teacher cornered me to share the "hit report." I felt very alone, as I would try to respond appropriately. *Should I apologize for his behavior to the parent of the child Ollie hurt? To Ollie's teacher? Should I suggest a different plan for redirecting Ollie?* Sustaining the emotional impact of the hit report became more challenging with each day. I began to dread pickup.

This was one year before the preschool teacher would say that she didn't know how to help Ollie anymore, two years before he would be diagnosed with sensory processing disorder, three years before the second preschool would try to kick him out, and four years before we would learn that he was on the autism spectrum. I didn't know then that the hit report was just the beginning. That over the next five years, my stress, the demands on my time, and my rage were going to balloon from the effort it would take to single-handedly force the healthcare system and the school system to provide my kid with the intensive and specialized support he needed—all while trying to parent a child who was behaving in ways I didn't understand.

That day, all I knew was I hated the look on the teacher's face as she made a beeline for me through the playground. I resented the pressure on me to "fix the problem." Weren't the teachers the childcare experts? I was just a lady who pushed out a baby. I felt so unprepared. *How do I get Ollie to control his body's urges? How can I teach him to use words instead?* I squeezed my vocabulary to fit into Ollie's: "No hitting," "Teeth are only for food," "We give hugs, not ouchies." Ollie would nod like he understood, but every day was the same. *Why can't I help him?* I felt ineffectual, and at the very heart of it, I was afraid. *Is something wrong with my kid?*

When Ollie went boneless in the street, my anxiety and fear spiked. His unusual and sometimes dangerous bodily impulses had been relatively contained by the safety of our home and his preschool. But out in the Wild West of street crossing, I was witness to how Ollie's behaviors could put him in harm's way, and it terrified me. On top of this, my emotional rollercoaster moment was on display. As drivers sat in their idling cars, watching us through their windshields, my pride morphed into pressure. Motherhood is so public, and everyone has an opinion. The man yelling at me from his car, the woman shooting me a nasty look— motherhood is an equal opportunity punching bag game. You don't even have to be a mother to play. In the world of motherhood, misogyny cloaks itself as judgment and ridicule, and it is impossible not to internalize it. Every eye on me was a spotlight as the announcer blared in my head: "Will the mother regain control over her child?"

But I was not thinking about the sexist pressures of modern motherhood, or the ways our healthcare and school systems fail children who have special needs. Instead, I was wondering how on earth I was going to tell Paul what happened. *Ollie stopped walking in the middle of the street, and I hulked out on him?* That wouldn't go over well. Even with the broader context, it would've sounded like an attempt to justify my behavior: *I might have hurt our kid, but I was feeling overwhelmed and undersupported, and exposed and judged as a mother.* The basement adds necessary information to the mom rage story, but it never excuses our actions.

That day was a wake-up call. Soon I'd be in individual therapy, couples therapy, life coaching, and anger management. I'd receive a medical diagnosis, see body workers, try antidepressants and antianxiety medications. I would do all the things to try to stop raging.

Paul was only too familiar with the anger that burst into our lives not long after Ollie came along. But this new realization that

I could be *so* out of control, *so* careless with little Ollie's pudding self? It was more than I could bear saying out loud.

The silence that surrounds mom rage is filled with fear. This fear gets instilled in us through cultural messaging that tells us motherhood is just the best. And if anyone dare disagree? Shame! We worry if our shameful words hit the air, our monstrousness might be true. So many of us struggling with mom rage don't tell our partners. We are afraid our friends will think badly of us, or they won't relate. We are terrified that if we share how furious we've become since having babies, it will get twisted into "I hate being a mom," which will further twist into "I don't love my children."

At the end of a rage-filled day, we lie in bed curled in a fetal position, sobbing. We think of the softness of our babies' skin, the way our children have a deep knowing that our bodies are nests, and they snuggle in till everything's just right, like a cat turning circles before she settles down. Not loving our children? This couldn't be further from the truth. But the fear that someone might misunderstand takes our breath away. So we retreat—into our beds, our cars, our drinks, our screens, ourselves. We shut the windows. We lock the doors. We don't tell a soul.

2 THE SCAM OF MOTHERHOOD

I have the best husband. . . . He just doesn't antici-
pate all of the needs of our family like I do. So I'm
always going to lose a little bit unless I let things
go to shit. And I can't let things go to shit because
I have a child. And I'm so pissed off about that. I
love him, and I married the best that you can . . .
of men. I married a sensitive, smart, funny, hand-
some, evolved, liberated man, and still I cannot
fucking fight the imbalance, and it drives me out
of my mind.

—Jennifer Romolini, *Everything Is Fine* podcast

Motherhood has a top-notch public relations team.
They coax us: "Motherhood is so rewarding." They as-
sure us: "Children will take care of you when you're old." They
scare us: "You'll regret it if you don't have children." These
talking points, endorsed by everyone from celebrities and media
figures to politicians to our own mothers, add up to a massive

propaganda machine that promotes the PR team's best-selling pitch: "Motherhood is the best job a woman can have." With no pay, no health insurance, no assistants, no vacation, no 401(k), no professional development, no promotions, and a toxic, sink-or-swim environment, it's certainly not the best job *I've* ever had. Despite the position's unattractive attributes, mothers are shackled to the job with golden handcuffs because we love our "clients" so damn much.

I'm just going to say it: Motherhood is a scam.

When I say *motherhood*, I'm not talking about people birthing babies or caring for them. People with uteruses have been re-populating the human race for eons, long before concepts like motherhood and mothering existed. I'll get to this soon.

What I'm talking about is today's capital-M Motherhood—a totalizing identity that subsumes the person you used to be under the new and all-encompassing life purpose of bringing up good and useful humans, and being nothing other than (or at least nothing *nearly* as important as) Mom.

The scam of Motherhood is in the shine campaign—*Get married, have babies, win womanhood!*—used to indoctrinate little girls. Careful not to reveal the scam at its heart, the PR team's campaign never mentions that in order to win at Motherhood, mothers must sacrifice their bodily and financial autonomy. Once we've won, we are further indoctrinated to believe that devoting every fiber of our being, every minute of our time, and every thought in our head to children and family is the natural way of things, that this is just what Motherhood is, and it's exactly what we signed up for. It must be, because there is no way to keep up with the demands of modern Motherhood if we have full and interesting lives outside of mothering. If we're sad that Motherhood has replaced our once robust lives with cleaning out the crevices of tiny Tupperware containers and giving a thousand performances of *Goodnight Moon*, the PR team tells us our melancholy is our own fault, and we really need to "work on our self-care." The scam of Motherhood is implanted so deeply inside us that when we inevitably don't live up to its unending demands, we blame ourselves.

Writer Adrienne Rich called capital-M Motherhood "the patriarchal institution of motherhood," meaning that the experience of modern motherhood has been so co-opted by patriarchy that motherhood as we know it today is mostly in service to men and the systems that prioritize men (especially, I'd note, white cis men). The uniquely intimate and tender relationship between a mother and her children gets overshadowed by the sheer volume of work that is almost entirely on the mother's shoulders but benefits the father and the society.

Motherhood's PR team tells mothers we must throw ourselves full throttle into our mothering job—researching, planning, contacting, scheduling, overseeing, washing, tidying, folding, driving, thanking, inviting, hosting, cooking, preparing, and sharing. All this unpaid labor of caring for children, spouses, and everything else in the domestic sphere frees up fathers to bring their most focused selves to their jobs, rise in the workforce, and access their creative and professional potential because mothers are *holding it down!** This is the scam of Motherhood.

The unspoken avalanche of responsibilities doesn't just exhaust mothers and make them feel resentful, it sabotages their professional lives. In a 2009 PEW Research Center study, women were more than four times as likely as men to say they don't work because their partner doesn't want them to. Even when women work jobs outside the home, they don't get to focus fully on their careers the way fathers do because mothers are still the primary parent.

---

* See "How Partners Benefit Professionally from Mothers Being the Primary Parent" in the Appendix.

US Bureau of Labor statistics from 2021 show that women were nearly twice as likely as men to work only part time. Of those women, 82 percent said they worked part time for non-economic reasons, like shouldering family responsibilities.

Whether moms are high-powered lawyers earning more than their partners or stay-at-home moms who can't afford the high cost of childcare, they are still the ones up at night on the internet, ordering the next size shoe for the children, signing them up for the next session of after-school care, and researching the best occupational therapist for their needs. Instead of inventing new mechanical creations or writing the next great American novel— or just allowing ourselves to deeply rest—we are using all our energy, creative and otherwise, to keep up with the demands of the job of Motherhood.

The more we do, the less our partners need to do. Many mothers I spoke to said their husbands were really great men and "the best father," but also admitted their husbands seemed to not notice the things that need doing in their homes and for their children. When mothers did point these things out, asking their husbands to clean the dirty pan or pack the diaper bag for the outing, the husbands would do a subpar job. Because our gendered upbringing tends to prime boys for the skills of fatherhood (earning money, doing physically demanding home maintenance like mowing the lawn or cleaning the gutters, and playing sports with the kids on the weekends), dads often fall short on the everyday skills of parenting. This puts the onus on mothers to either pick up their husband's slack or do the painstaking work of teaching their husband how to parent.

Most of the mothers I interviewed in same-sex marriages acknowledged that because one of them was the primary parent, an uneven labor split existed in their household. Unlike the moms in different-sex marriages, when moms in same-sex marriages complained, they did not feel the need to first show their loyalty to their spouse by adding the disclaimer that she is "the best mother." Mothers in same-sex marriages tended not to experience the same lack of childcare and housework skills in their spouses.

Some of the mothers married to men, on the other hand, described their husbands as their third child. Motherhood's PR team makes light of this phenomenon through the bumbling husband trope on television. Today's Gen X and millennial dads grew up watching Homer Simpson and the bumbling fathers on *Family Guy* and *Home Improvement*. A 2020 study analyzed scenes of TV dads from 1980 to 2017 and discovered that over time TV dads are appearing in key parenting scenes less and less often. And when they *are* shown, the study describes their parenting as "humorously foolish." But on TV, the mother character doesn't rage at the injustice of it. Instead, she accepts her husband's ineptitude—which is actually his refusal to do 50 percent of the work—by making a face and patting him lovingly on the head before bringing him back in line or doing the work for him.

Lauren, forty-six, an Anglo-Australian theater artist and mother to a twelve-year-old boy, described her British travel agent husband as "a bit of a grown-up boy." She identified this as a key source of her mom rage. "We got married, had a baby, and for us that meant I was essentially going to become my husband's parenting coach, and sort of quasi-parent." Lauren's husband comes from a conservative British military family, and his own father "is quite proud to announce he's never changed a nappy [diaper]." Lauren said her husband's "heart is in the right place," but she still felt tasked with having to teach him the emotional, social, and practical aspects of raising a child. As Lauren got angrier and more ground down by this additional labor, she started questioning it, wondering, "Why is it my role to do this? It's taking away from my ability to have my own pursuits and desires, because I've got this massive project of coaching my partner to be a twenty-first-century parent."

One could argue that mothers who are fed up should just refuse to teach their husbands how to parent and let them figure it out for themselves. But the reality is mothers are in a bind of the patriarchy's creation. Lauren doesn't want the additional labor of teaching her partner how to parent—no one explicitly taught *her*—but she also doesn't want their son to have an inept parent. Either she loses or her child loses. The issue is her husband's, yet the predicament is Lauren's. If mothers are set up to either teach their male partners how to parent, or more likely, throw their hands up in exasperation and do most of the work themselves because it is the less exhausting option in the short term, what is the incentive for dads to do half of the parenting labor? The status quo of Motherhood is serving *their* interests just fine. But what is left of *us*?

Mothers end up exhausted or seething with frustration. It's a confounding anger when there is no exact *who* to be mad at. Instead of the invisible PR team, we see our own selves, who seemingly have allowed our lives to be swallowed whole by Motherhood. We see our partners who we mostly still adore, despite their blissful unawareness of the myriad ways our unending work advantages them. We see our children who, despite their selective hearing and rollercoaster emotions, delight us with their squishy knees and fresh musings about the world. We are unsure we even have a right to be angry. *You are so blessed*, the PR team reminds us whenever we dare to lodge a complaint. Stuck inside the scam of "the best job a woman can have," we do not know where or at whom to direct our shamed fury.

In her foreword to the 2021 reprint of Adrienne Rich's seminal book *Of Woman Born*, Eula Biss describes how the complex experience of being a loving mom within the patriarchal institution of motherhood leads to mom rage:

The emotional experience of mothering is among the richest possibilities that motherhood offers. But everything we feel for our children—the tenderness, the awe and delight—can become entangled with everything we feel about the institution of motherhood. That institution is so diffuse, so widespread, so lacking a central office, so without an identifiable authority, that the rage we feel about being trapped within it is sometimes directed, for lack of another outlet, at our own children.

The power of Motherhood's PR is in its insidious ubiquity. The ideas are in the water we guzzle every day. We drink it down in the name of hydration and call it "self-care" until we think the ideas are our own: *Lil John-John's too young to go to daycare all day. He should be with his mom. I think I'll stay home till he's two.*

In her famous 1981 keynote address, "The Uses of Anger," Audre Lorde talks about a similar kind of PR team for white supremacy, which she calls "mainstream communication." She says, "Mainstream communication does not want women, particularly white women, responding to racism. It wants racism to be accepted as an immutable given in the fabric of existence, like evening time or the common cold." Similarly, the PR team does not welcome voices responding to the scam of Motherhood. Dissenting voices bring bad publicity to Motherhood, which, like white supremacy, is supposed to be assumed—so normalized we don't notice it, let alone the injustice of it.

Just as white people aren't inherently smarter than people of color, women and people with uteruses aren't inherently better suited for child-rearing. Yet Western cultural messaging has convinced us otherwise. Fifty-one percent of Americans believe children are better off with mothers who stay home and don't work, while only 8 percent say the same of fathers. We may know

that the concepts and meanings of Motherhood are socially constructed, but we've bought into them as the dominant cultural
narrative, making their day-to-day lived experience very real.
Many of us may agree that the modern system of Motherhood
does not benefit moms, yet 83 percent of stay-at-home parents are
mothers.

Motherhood and its cultural meanings are mutable. The dominant philosophy of mothering today in the US is *intensive mothering*, a term coined by Sharon Hays in her 1996 book *The Cultural
Contradictions of Motherhood*. She describes intensive mothering as "child-centered, expert-guided, emotionally absorbing,
labor-intensive, and financially expensive." Intensive mothering
came onto the parenting scene as use of the internet was becoming more common and widespread. As a result, intensive mothering has that same omnipresent feel: *always be mothering*. This
ideology is what causes parents to track the length of our babies'
naps with an app, click "Buy Now" for the latest parenting book,
and spend every Saturday morning at toddler soccer.

Intensive mothering is pervasive, and its expectations infiltrate
the minds of moms and non-moms alike. When mothers try to
push back against intensive mothering by not signing their children up for extracurriculars or refusing to surveil their children
every second of every day, the culture claps back. "Motherhood
is policed," writes Eula Biss, "both informally and formally, by
mothers as well as people who are not mothers—by joggers and
judges and bystanders and actual police officers."

Elizabeth, a white middle-class community college professor of
English who lives in Seattle with her wife and their two children,
experienced this sort of policing when she loosened her parenting leash for just a moment. She was walking back from the park
with her kids when her five-year-old son started running ahead.
Elizabeth did the mental calculations: *We're only two blocks from the*

house. He knows where the house is. These are not busy streets. He's not acting out of control. Almost immediately, a car pulled over. A man leaned out the window and asked if everything was okay. Elizabeth told me that it's hard for her to make her own parenting decisions because she feels like everywhere she goes, "there's this army of enforcers. There's this cultural mandate to be hypervigilant." Perhaps the man was just being a good Samaritan looking out for a young child. Regardless, his inclination to step in and Elizabeth's hesitancy to let her son run ahead are both the results of the current intensive mothering moment we are in that tells us children must be watched and attended to by their parents at all times.

The parenting ideologies that were swirling around in popular culture when I was having kids in the 2010s were all versions of intensive mothering. There was *helicopter parenting*: always be watching, always be near. There was *attachment parenting*: never put the baby down—wear them, sleep with them, nurse them till kindergarten. And there was the *tiger mom*, which has its origins in Chinese American immigrant parenting, but whose principles have since filtered into the culturally dominant, white middle-class story of modern Motherhood. To be a tiger mom is to make sure your kids are in all the right programs for academic success and eventual upward class mobility. In the past few years, *gentle parenting* has become popular. It espouses that when a child acts out, parents should pause and get down on a child's eye level and question, examine, and process the child's behavior together—while doing their best to not let on that the child's behavior makes them want to scratch their eyes out. Each of these parenting philosophies is just as Sharon Hays described in 1996: expert-guided, emotionally absorbing, labor-intensive, and financially expensive.

No matter what her approach, the modern mom doesn't just "lean in" to the job. She throws herself off the high dive, then desperately treads water for the next eighteen or so years: hosting themed birthday parties she researched on Pinterest; signing the kids up for violin, basketball, and Spanish; evaluating vegan diet options and vaccine schedules; performing as her family's tech programmer, psychiatrist, medic, travel agent, researcher, cook, stylist, chauffer, wilderness leader, and modern-day switchboard operator. ("Ollie, Grant's calling to video chat!") And on top of her all-consuming job of Mother, she's likely one of the roughly 80 percent of moms who also have full-time *paid* jobs.

As someone who is aware that Motherhood is a feat of social engineering, I'd like to think I'm onto the PR team and their tricks. But I'm susceptible too. "I don't read parenting books," I say proudly, like I'm punk rock or something. But actually, there was that one book Paul and I refer to as "the sleep bible"—the one with the dog-eared pages I desperately read and reread in between watching TV shows at full volume, trying to drown out Ollie's cries, then his sister Mae's four years later, during the dreaded sleep-training periods. Then there was that one popular book we bought when Ollie was having what we thought were behavioral issues at his first preschool. And I guess I did buy that book about extreme food pickiness, when strawberries and Cheerios were all we could get down his gullet for two years. So even someone like me, who identifies as being allergic to parenting advice, ended up joining the hordes of American millennial moms who spend an estimated annual $231.6 million on parenting books and $141 million on apps to help us parent "better."

When I became a mother, I didn't know there was a grand PR narrative of Motherhood to buy into or resist. Intensive mothering had infiltrated the parenting world I stepped into so completely, I couldn't see it. It was, as Lorde says, "an immutable given in the fabric of existence." My life became completely child-centered the moment my babies crawled on stage. Even still, our weekends are dedicated to the children. You can find my family at local playgrounds, other kids' birthday parties, public pools when it's hot, or maybe the Oakland Zoo if we shelled out for a membership that year. We quit restaurants because our children are tyrants who only eat bread anyway, and we stopped going to museums because who can enjoy art when you're sprinting after children screaming, "Don't touch!" as they run up and lick the paintings? I don't consciously subscribe to any ideologies that preach this is the right way to parent. Intellectually, I'd say the child should join the parents' lives, not the other way around. But it just *happened*.

I was sure it was my own personal preferences that prompted me to make baby food purees from scratch rather than buying the same food in a jar off the supermarket shelf. I got satisfaction from blending fruits and vegetables and pouring the purees into ice cube trays, filling my freezer with baby food rainbows. We lived in the major metropolis of San Francisco when Ollie was born, but making baby food made me feel like I was canning homemade jam or something. It was my DIY homesteader moment! I didn't love cleaning every piece of the stupid food mixer, but I felt proud. *Look what a good mother I am—making, feeding, storing, nourishing.*

Wearing my babies in a carrier on my body all day long made sense too. They cried less, plus their warm little bodies felt so good! I was proud of my "ability" to birth without an epidural or other pain relief measures—before I ever had babies in my arms, I was eager to suffer to show my strength as a "good" mother. The PR team tells us these are natural, and therefore superior, ways of mothering. Cloth diapers (natural!) made a huge comeback in the 2000s, much to the horror of 1950s and 1960s mothers who rejoiced at the invention of disposable diapers. You know what cloth diapering, constant babywearing, drug-free birthing, and making homemade baby food all have in common? They are labor-intensive mothering methods. If I'm wearing my kid all day, steaming, pureeing, then freezing his food, laundering every diaper, and breastfeeding until twelve or twenty-four months, you know what I'm not doing? Anything else!

Two foundational tenets of Motherhood's presiding cultural narrative are that the mother is the natural and exclusive caregiver, and intensive mothering is good mothering. But these ideas aren't natural at all. If we follow these narratives back to their origins and before, we see they are stories created to uphold the interests of men.

In the Middle Ages, European mothers were not seen as containing some supreme maternal instinct that better suited them for child-rearing. Fathers and mothers shared parenting duties equally, and childcare was not thought of as intrinsically good work; it was seen as burdensome. Parents who could afford it sent their babies to be cared for by wet nurses for up to three years. Kids were considered economic assets and put to work as early as age six or seven. In the American colonies, the Puritans influenced the approach to child-rearing; instead of being ignored, children became forms for both parents to mold. (Remnants of this idea exist in today's intensive mothering.) The few parenting manuals available in the seventeenth and eighteenth centuries were written for fathers or sometimes for parents in general, but rarely were they specifically addressed to mothers. Mothers were not revered for their parenting ability but for their fertility. Physically producing a child was a fundamentally separate undertaking from raising one.

Up until the Industrial Revolution, work and home were a single-family enterprise. As families abandoned farm life for cities and men left the home to earn wages in factories, the two worlds split. The work of the home became the mother's domain, particularly for middle-class families who could survive finan-cially without a second income. Fathers benefited from mothers caring for the children and house, just as they do today. It elimi-nated mothers from job competition and freed fathers of domestic responsibilities.

As the work/home divide grew wider, dominant cultural views about children and mothers changed. Children came to be seen as precious, innocent beings in need of protection. Childcare be-came virtuous, honorable work, and by default, mothering took on a similar golden sheen. By the second half of the nineteenth century, "child-rearing" meant "mothering."

Children's newfound cultural purity extended into the domains of play and creativity around the turn of the twentieth century. Childhood was considered to be a special time, which resulted in the establishment of a play-based year of instruction called kin-dergarten, and the beginning of the playground movement, when thousands of dedicated recreation spaces—outdoor gymnasiums, ice skating rinks, "sand piles" in public parks—were constructed across America as healthy alternatives to the vacant lots and back alleys where kids used to play. By the 1960s, playgrounds (like mothers) were expected to do the imagination work *for* children, with their rocket ships and animal-shaped play structures.

The playground movement was a harbinger of present-day intensive expectations of mothers: *Always be playing! Make it fun!* I don't find playgrounds very fun. Occasionally they serve as a venue to meet a fellow mom friend, but that only happens when Venus and Saturn align at the stroke of midnight on the twenty-eighth day of the seventh month of the year. Even if the stars do align, letting my guard down at playgrounds has never felt feasible, even with Mae, who seems neurotypical so far. Once Mae got old enough to play independently without falling on her face, I learned the hard way (twice) that if I don't spot her every few minutes, she aimlessly walks away. This is why I dress her in neon.

Do I sound overbearing? I didn't walk into motherhood this way. Ollie was only two when *play*ground started to feel like a misnomer. I learned to be an eagle-eyed observer, at the ready with reminders to be gentle or to ask before touching another child. I experienced other parents, friends even, staring at me with that "Jeez, lady, he's fine" look. But what those parents didn't know is what would happen when I wasn't vigilant, when I slacked on my "job," when I enjoyed my coffee and focused on my grown-up friend—on my own pleasure—too much. That's when an elbow would connect with a face. That's when Ollie would shove a kid to the ground. That's when the crying would start, the apologizing, the checking, the separating, the meltdown, the leaving, the utter exhaustion, the frustration, the overwhelm, and sometimes the rage.

Those parents giving the "jeez" look didn't know that's what awaited me when I let my guard down, when I tried to be one of those French mommies Pamela Druckerman describes in *Bringing Up Bébé*, the ones who don't overparent like American moms do. I have so many judging voices in my head. My French mommy voice says, *Relax. Look at your phone, talk to your friend, drink your coffee, smoke your fantasy cigarette. Your kid doesn't need to play with you. That's the whole point of a playground!* I'd like to give those cool, French mommies my child to contend with, and see how chic and chill *they* are an hour later.

Only recently, now that Ollie is nine and Mae is five, have I been able to channel my inner French mommy, sipping coffee on a bench with a mom friend—or more likely by myself because Mercury was in retrograde or one of us got pink eye again. It's likely my French cool won't last long because one of my kids will want me to play with them, and up I'll go to the top of the rope tower, playing pirate. "Arg!" So, okay, I'm never going to be the aloof French mommy.

As an American, the mothering style of the archetypal French mom feels unnatural to me, but American parenting norms from just a century ago are almost inconceivable. In a section of the US government's 1914 pamphlet *Infant Care*, called "Playing with the Baby," it reads, "The rule that parents should not play with the baby may seem hard, but it is without doubt a safe one."

As cultural norms change, parenting expectations shift with them. Today's intensive mothering encourages us to mold our little humans to be just as moral, smart, and proper as a good nineteenth-century child and as creative, friendly, and skilled as a twentieth-century one, not to mention our own century's additions of emotionally intelligent, open-minded, and kind.

Parents not playing with their children isn't just an old-timey anecdote, it's what I remember from my own childhood. Sure, my parents played cards with me, but they didn't cut my sandwiches into miniature hearts, build forts, or engage in hours of pretend play with me. In her viral essay, "The New Midlife Crisis," Ada Calhoun reminds us that many of today's parents born between 1965 and 1980 had parents who didn't prioritize that kind of focused engagement. Calhoun writes, "As one Gen X woman tells me, her boomer mother comes to visit and is mystified. 'Why do you play with them?' her mother asks. 'We never played with you.'"

Author, academic, and founder of Demeter Press ("the first press on motherhood, reproduction, sexuality, and the family"), Andrea O'Reilly calls this relaxed phase of boomer-generation parenting in the 1980s "custodial mothering." Author and professor Tatjana Takseva describes custodial mothering as "very much a hands-off kind of motherhood in the sense that children would be sent out to play in the street with their friends for indeterminate amounts of time. There was never any expectation that adults were responsible for entertaining children."

Born in 1981, I am the "Xennial" child of boomer parents. (Xennials are the micro-generation in between Gen X and millennials, born between 1979 and 1983.) When my parents fly from Philadelphia to the Bay Area to visit me and my family, I am thrilled to see them. We hug tightly at the airport and I think, *I wish I didn't live so far from them.* By day three, the difference between their custodial mothering and my intensive mothering is in sharp relief. I sit on the living room floor playing with toys with Mae, narrating what I'm doing and what she's doing, praising her, kissing her. Ollie is on his own in another room conducting his Lego fantasy world. My parents watch me play with Mae, their bottoms permanently imprinted on our hand-me-down leather sofas. They are perfectly happy to occasionally interact with my kids—from their seats.

Play with them, I plead in my head. *Be Fun Grandma and Fun Grandpa.* But they're mostly not, even as they send gifts and love love love my children. I don't know why I'm surprised. They weren't Fun Mom or Fun Dad either, and it never, not once, bothered me. I have always felt loved and protected, encouraged and adored. My parents played with me in the ways *they* liked to play—puzzles and hopscotch with Mom, card games and catch with Dad. Much of the time I was on my own. I spent hours of my childhood alone in the back alleyways of West Philadelphia, playing detective, finding "clues" (broken glass hulls of 40-oz. bottles of Colt 45).

Decades after rattling around like Junior Mints in the way back of a station wagon, eighties babies like me are perhaps course-correcting for the moments we felt underparented in our own childhoods. My generation has grown into today's intensive mothers, who know the pros and cons of six brands of car seats.

Staying on top of the colossal demands of modern Motherhood nearly requires graduate-level knowledge, which comes with a graduate-level price tag. But what kind of mothers are able to participate in this time-consuming, high-cost mothering?

Today, advertising and consumer culture reach most people across the globe, including low-income mothers. Motherhood's PR team uses media to tell consumers (everyone) what the job of Mother entails. Imagine a commercial for laundry detergent: the mother launders her children's soiled clothes—a grass-stained soccer uniform and a dirt-covered outfit from mud-play in the backyard. According to this commercial, a mother who is doing the job right (intensively) signs her kids up for soccer lessons and allows her children the pleasure of rolling around in mud, despite the time and energy it will cost her to clean the stains (not to mention the children themselves). It also presumes that she is the one who does her family's laundry in their single-family home, which contains their own washer and dryer and a backyard—all signifiers of middle-class financial success.

In her essay "How Contemporary Consumerism Shapes Intensive Mothering," Takseva calls intensive mothering a "privileged ideology" that assumes most moms have extra money to spend on their children. She explains that even though poor and working-class mothers may not be financially able to provide their children with all the same experiences as middle-class or wealthy mothers, they receive the same Motherhood messaging, and as a result, "continue to view the same as desirable and somehow beneficial to children." Unattainable Motherhood standards, created to uphold white middle-class, capitalist, patriarchal ideals, leave mothers of all socioeconomic backgrounds to battle through feelings of inadequacy and guilt, and potentially anger.

In one of my interviews, a mom named Zaara told me it didn't take long for the ceaseless demands of Motherhood to make her feel overwhelmed and subsequently angry. Zaara was thirty years old when two girls, sisters, aged eight and four at the time, were placed to live with her and her husband. Back in college, Zaara and her husband agreed that if they got married, they'd make a family by taking in foster kids. "We were idealistic college kids back then," Zaara laughed. But later on, when Zaara worked as a teacher, she found herself wanting to take home many of her students who were in foster care. So, when she and her husband were ready to start a family, "that was just the way we decided to go," Zaara said.

Zaara identifies as South Asian and her husband is Turkish. They are middle class and Muslim, living in Minneapolis, Minnesota. Their daughters are Black. When the four of them became a family, Zaara's husband was working full time as a project manager in tech. Zaara was working on a PhD in educational curriculum design.

She described the way they shared childcare and domestic labor during the beginning of their parenting journey as "pretty evenly split, because we were both full-time busy." They had a schedule for who was in charge of making or picking up dinner, and another schedule for school pickups and drop-offs. "Because I was a PhD student," Zaara explained, "my schedule was always a little more flexible, so I did more of the in-person stuff—doctor appointments and things like that." If Zaara had appointments for the girls during the day, her husband would take over the bedtime routine so she could get some of her work done in the evenings.

But after two semesters with the girls staying in after-school programming until six o'clock, the couple felt they weren't getting to know their children, so they made some adjustments. "Because I made less money as a grad student and was also less committed to it than [my husband] was to his job, I took a leave of absence."

One could argue that Zaara made a "choice" to leave her job, despite being an educated, career-oriented woman who never wanted to be a stay-at-home mom. The PR team would say she did this to be a better mother. One could even describe Zaara's "choice" as logical, since she wasn't the breadwinning parent. But when we look at all the families making the same "choice," we see that it is not just a personal decision but a systemic funneling that incentivizes two-parent families in which one parent (almost always the father or masculine partner) works and makes the money, and the second parent (almost always the mother or femme partner) stays home and does the child-rearing and domestic labor.

In half of families in America, the mother is the breadwinner. But that statistic includes many households headed by single mothers. When we look only at mothers who are married to men, just 20 to 33 percent are breadwinners. This is because of the PR team's pressure on mothers to be with our children constantly, even to the detriment of our careers and our selfhood. It's also because of the gender wage gap, which exists in many countries around the world. In the US, on average, women earn 82 cents for every dollar earned by men. The wage gap is widest for most women of color.

Motherhood further diminishes women's earning potential. In the United States, on average, mothers earn just sixty-nine cents for every dollar earned by fathers. That's a 13 percent motherhood penalty *on top* of the 18 percent penalty for being a woman. And while mothers' salaries decrease with each additional child, dads benefit from a "fatherhood bonus," their salaries rising with each child. One British study put that pay increase at 21 percent.

A woman doesn't even need to be a mother to suffer from the motherhood wage penalty. In 2019, a German research institute conducted a study on gender discrimination against job applicants.

The study found that married women with no children received the least number of callbacks, proving that the very *possibility* of pregnancy and babies was seen as the biggest threat to women's productivity, and resulted in "substantial hiring discrimination." Just the threat that a person *might* become a mother can cost her.

Depending on a variety of factors including race, class, and geographical location, the combination of the gender wage gap and the motherhood penalty results in moms losing anywhere from $10,500 to $98,000 annually. This lifelong devaluation of a mother's earnings gets ignored—and tossed onto the piles in the mom rage basement—when both parents agree that it "makes sense" for the mom to sacrifice her work (just for a year . . . or two . . . or forever) to stay home with the children.

"Circumstances conspire on every level to get [mothers] to fall back in this traditional role," said Robert-Jay Green, professor emeritus at the California School of Professional Psychology in San Francisco, in an interview in the *New York Times*. "Once you have children, it starts to almost pressure the couple into this kind of division of labor, and we're seeing this now even in same-sex couples." What's different with same-sex couples, though, says Stephanie Coontz, author of *Marriage: A History*, is that they are "less likely than different-sex couples to assign 'women's work' to the partner with fewer work hours. They are also more likely to talk through their individual preferences about who does what at home."

For many partnered mothers, especially those partnered to men, *not* leaving their paid jobs and attempting to split domestic work and childcare equitably ends up being *more* work than acquiescing to the cultural tide that pushes them out of the workforce and into the home. Either way, the job of primary parent—often just called "Mother"—is constant, invisible, and unacknowledged labor.

For example, those schedules Zaara and her husband used to make their division of labor "pretty evenly split"? Zaara made them. "It wouldn't occur to my husband otherwise," she said. "I put kid events in our shared Google Calendar and include who's in charge in the details." For busier weeks, Zaara creates a Google Doc that she shares with her husband. It includes appointments, practices, work schedules, plans for meals, and any additional help they might need for childcare.

Unsurprisingly, when Zaara took a leave of absence from her PhD program, the division of domestic labor became more unbalanced. "It was pretty much all on me . . . but he helped." As per the schedule, Zaara's husband made meals three or four days a week. He cleaned up after all the dinners. He made a concerted effort to contribute, yet the primary-parent train tracks had already been laid. Many of us don't see the tracks or realize we're heading out of a somewhat equal distribution of labor into an unequal one until it's too late. Here's how the progression happened for Zaara and her husband, as Zaara told it:

- The kids felt more comfortable with me, telling me what was going on, so I was more likely to be the one dealing with social workers, psychiatrists, therapists, etc.
- People would email me and not [their dad]. I wouldn't realize they hadn't included him in the conversation.
- [After taking a leave of absence from my PhD program] I had more time during the day, so I'd respond, then be surprised later that [my husband] was totally out of the loop.
- If something went wrong at school, they'd call mom. If the kids' caseworker needed some paperwork, they would call or email me, because they assumed that [their dad] wouldn't have that information.
- Over time [this came true]. He just wouldn't have it.

- I got so much of the background information from those informal conversations at school pickups/drop-offs and at doctor appointments, that keeping [my husband] looped in was
  more work than just taking care of it myself.

In addition to the boulder of labor that rests on the backs of
every primary parent, Zaara had the additional work of learning
who her daughters were, how to navigate their complex needs,
and settling them into their new home. Both suffered acute
trauma before they were fostered and ultimately adopted by Zaara
and her husband. The girls struggle with a host of challenges including ADHD, dyslexia, self-harming, and PTSD. It's standard
that during the first few months of a new foster care placement,
various professionals will drop by the house to make sure the
children are adjusting and check that the home is a suitable environment. Because of the girls' past trauma, any time an adult—a
caseworker, or even a friend of the family—would come into the
house, the girls would have meltdowns, which Zaara described
as "crying in corners, or being really attached to us, or attacking
the person verbally or kicking them." Someone would stop by for
thirty minutes to make sure their fire alarms were working, and
then it would take the parents "four hours to get everybody set-
tled down and reassured."

On top of visits with their caseworkers, therapy sessions, and
the mountain of appointments the girls needed for starting new
schools, there was always something popping up that would take
much of Zaara's time and emotional energy. An unknown nut al-
lergy landed one daughter in the hospital. Another had an asthma
attack. "At least two or three times a week, we were running
to do something along those medical or mental health lines."
All of this was in addition to baseline parenting time commit-
ments, like attending school holiday concerts and parent-teacher

conferences. "It was a lot," Zaara sighed. Babysitters were out of the question. Talking about her younger daughter, Zaara said, "No one else can really watch her . . . even still [four years later], it's just not really doable."

The girls had sleep issues, which all mothers know means Zaara had sleep issues. Between the sleep deprivation, the continuous string of emergencies, and the stress of holding everything together, Zaara started experiencing rage. "I don't know that I even recognized that what I felt was rage. As I got more used to my kids, I would get really angry at them because, I mean, they're kids, so they'd mess up. And because of some of their needs, they'd mess up kind of big." Zaara would watch the clock when her husband was at work, waiting for the moment he'd arrive home so she could get a break. Sometimes he'd be "an extra half hour late because he got stuck in traffic, or it'd snow, and I would explode at him."

Zaara's rage got so bad that for five or six months, she was yelling at the girls nonstop, then directly following the rage, she would fall asleep. She began experiencing chronic back pain and a stress gag response. "I could barely brush my teeth because I was going to vomit. I was eating junk food all the time. None of that felt good."

Zaara didn't realize her rage was related to anxiety until she was filling out a generalized anxiety disorder checklist at the hospital for her daughter. "I answered *Yes* [for myself] on everything. It just didn't occur to me that being up at night worrying about things wasn't normal. My mom was also like that." And Zaara's rage episodes followed by sleeping? A therapist and a doctor told her they were likely panic attacks.

While anger is a distinct emotional experience from anxiety, the two can merge into a tangle that makes us unsure if we're yelling angrily because we're truly mad or because we're brimming with anxiety. A 2021 study showed that people who have anger attacks—defined as "uncharacteristic sudden bouts of anger that are disproportionate to the situation"—are more likely to have elevated levels of anxiety and irritability. Women are twice as likely to suffer from severe stress and anxiety as men. This feels unsurprising to me, even inevitable. Just look at the way the bulk of the invisible labor fell into Zaara's lap. The circumstances were choreographed for her to step right into the primary parent role that was always waiting for her.

Women are raised to be detail-oriented and good at time management, coordination, and communication—essentially all the bits and pieces that must get taken care of. It's not the glory work, it's the grunt work that keeps the world turning. This continues right into motherhood. After the birth of a child, mothers are expected to be the parent who holds all the details: what the child eats, how much, what must be in the bag for daycare, what time the naps are, the babysitters' phone numbers. Mothers' own needs and details fall to the wayside as they struggle to stay on top of every single thing in their family's lives. This additional workload of overseeing all the details as the household manager and leading expert on their own children has been proven to directly decrease mothers' well-being.

The PR team is eerily silent about the darker aspects of Motherhood. They don't mention that our mental wellness is exponentially more likely to plummet and can remain that way for years, even decades. Or that refusing the role of primary parent and household manager is nearly impossible to do without feeling, and being perceived as, willfully neglectful, whereas when fathers put their jobs first, the waters part for these "good men." Or that the relentless workload of Motherhood that keeps us constantly on the move, even when our bodies are still, edges us ever closer to rage. Or that even though rage is a natural reaction to being systematically stripped of one's power, mothers can't actually claim that any of this is happening *to* us because we seemingly each made the "choice" to shrink our own lives. This keeps not only the PR team silent, but us too. Because who, exactly, can we blame besides ourselves? The PR team? What even *is* that? How can I get in touch with them?

Without public warning or even a whisper network, each mother is left to figure it out herself. What we figure out is that motherhood is not the story we've been fed. We have been duped. The scam of Motherhood becomes evident the minute our own needs show up. From maternal healthcare to childcare to eldercare, the failures of society's systems to take care of mothers persist for the rest of our lives. But we'd better keep our rage to ourselves, because motherhood is the best job a woman can have.

3 WHO CARES FOR THE CAREGIVER?

Rage is a kind of refusal. To be made a fool of, to be silenced, to be shamed, or to stand for anybody's bullshit.

—Brittney Cooper, *Eloquent Rage: A Black Feminist Discovers Her Superpower*

Before I left the hospital with a challah-sized Ollie in my arms, none of the staff mentioned to me that my poop would likely turn into jagged fossils that would claw my insides on their way out. This created an internal wound that wouldn't heal. It kept getting irritated because I kept on pooping, as humans do. I filled with dread every time I felt the urge. Each day I sat on the toilet and pushed my nails into the pads of my thumbs, gritted my teeth, and cried. I administered daily ointment up my anus for six months. Not to get too graphic—though motherhood is a messy, bloody, shit-filled experience—but I was still bleeding out of both holes at my six-week postpartum appointment, which was when my male doctor cheerfully announced I was cleared for sex with

Paul. Why was the emphasis on whether I could accommodate my husband's penis, and not on my painful, bleeding orifices? Why was the satisfaction of a man's (presumed) sexual desires the main talking point at *my* doctor appointment?

This focus on the penis, even in a maternal health setting, is a result of a healthcare system created by white cis men for themselves. Women weren't even *allowed* to be included in clinical trials until 1986, and it wasn't until 1993 that it became federally required to include women and people of color in clinical trials. Brown bodies and women's bodies have never been the health system's main concern. It's the reason the true structural anatomy of the clitoris wasn't discovered until 1998. It's why the National Institutes of Health didn't have a branch to study vulvas, vaginas, ovaries, and uteruses until 2014.

Maternal health is a valley of neglect. At the hospital they teach you how to diaper the baby, but they don't tell you what a healing vagina should feel like. Someone checks the baby's latch, but they don't teach mothers what to do when our nipples bleed. They make sure parents understand the healthy range for how often a baby pees and poops, but not how often is healthy for the mother to cry. If the baby is healthy, American moms are booted from the hospital a couple days after birth with some boat-sized maxi pads and the promise of a forthcoming bill. The medical system and the society at large see a healthy baby as the goal, not a healthy mother.

By the time I gave birth to Mae, in lieu of proper care structures, I'd learned how to take care of myself. Beginning with the first day of Mae's life, I took a stool softener every day. I didn't stop until she weaned at eighteen months old and I no longer had to give her every ounce of water in my body. This worked like a charm—no fossil claws. When I go to baby showers now, I gift an economy-sized bottle of stool softener. It may not be pretty, or a registry item, but it's one small thing I can offer in the face of a system that isn't focused on truly caring for birthing people.

I cannot make a list long enough to encapsulate all the ways mothers and birthing people are harmed by the structures that are supposed to support us in doing "the most important job in the world." Each step on the motherhood journey is another piece of evidence that mothers' well-being is at the bottom of the culture's priority list—from prejudiced, substandard prenatal and postpartum care with abysmal maternal health outcomes, to no federal family leave, to inaccessible mental health treatment, to the lack of affordable early childcare education, to inadequate public schools (particularly for marginalized kids and families), to the childcare black hole every day after school from three to six o'clock and all summer long.

The care infrastructure in the US is "Money or Mommy"—if families don't have the financial means to pay out of pocket for everything from medical expertise to childcare, the onus is on mothers to provide it. We rage because over and over the culture says to mothers, "*You* are the caregivers. We will not take care of you."

The refusal to invest in mothercare begins long before the baby is even born.

Twenty percent of the American childbearing population needs the assistance of the global fertility industry, which was valued at $26 billion in 2020. Yet insurance coverage for in vitro fertilization (IVF) and other related treatments is limited at best, making the endeavor prohibitively expensive and out of reach for many. This discriminatory lack of access disproportionately impacts women, the LGBTQ community, and poor people. Like abortion, infertility is an issue of reproductive justice. When birthing people want to self-actualize by *not* having a baby, the state won't ensure access to birth control or abortion. When birthing people want to self-actualize by *having* a baby, the state shrugs, "It's on you."

Studies show that people who struggle to conceive have elevated levels of depression, anxiety, and stress. A landmark study from the *Journal of Psychosomatic Obstetrics and Gynecology* found that infertile women's stress levels are on par with women living with cancer. In addition to the many documented health problems that stress contributes to, it also is a root cause of mom rage.

Joelle, a white middle-class British hairdresser, pined to be a mother for twenty years. At forty-three, after a decade of trying, she and her live-in boyfriend began their eight-year IVF journey. The cost of IVF varies widely country to country, so Joelle traveled from the UK to the Czech Republic for her first round of IVF. Then she tried again in Cyprus. Finally, she did three rounds in Spain. Spain is one of only a handful of European countries that allow women over age fifty to pursue IVF using donor eggs. Joelle was fifty-one when she gave birth to her daughter, now four years old.

Even though Joelle's journey to motherhood was long, expensive, and full of heartache, she found herself in the same predicament as many postpartum mothers who are alone all day with a baby—lonely, stressed, and raging. "I can't believe I [rage], because half the time I have to pinch myself that I have her." Moms who struggle to conceive, moms of children who had extended stays in the neonatal intensive care unit (NICU), and moms of sick, disabled, or neurodivergent kids all have increased stress levels that make them more prone to mom rage. Then, on top of that, because of their children's vulnerability, or because they dreamed so long, worked so hard, and paid so much money to have their children, these moms often experience excess amounts of shame and guilt after losing their tempers.

No matter how a person in the US gets pregnant, they are up against the reality of the country's maternal death rate of 23.8 per every 100,000 live births, which has been consistently on the rise for thirty-five years and is the worst of all industrialized nations. Compare that to Norway, whose 2019 maternal death rate was zero.

Tanya, a white middle-class stay-at-home mom in New Jersey, was a hair's breadth away from being counted in the US maternal death rate the year she gave birth to her second child. Weeks before her second baby was due, Tanya and her husband were about to leave the hospital after a routine appointment when a staff member realized they'd forgotten to check Tanya's blood pressure, and stopped the couple. Throughout her pregnancy Tanya's blood pressure had tested in the normal range, but that day, the last-minute check revealed it had skyrocketed. Tanya had an emergency C-section on the spot. Her high blood pressure was an indicator that she had preeclampsia.

Tanya was lucky the hospital staff realized their mistake, and she and her baby survived. With proper prenatal and postpartum care, dying from preeclampsia is mostly *preventable*, yet approximately 76,000 birthing people and 500,000 babies die annually from it. In the United States, it causes maternal death at three to four times the rate of other wealthy nations. Rural and low-income birthing people are particularly vulnerable to preeclampsia, as are disabled people, who are eleven times more likely to die during pregnancy and birth than those who are not disabled. Black and Native moms in the United States are about three times as likely to die during childbirth as white moms.

America's high maternal death rate is a symptom of a dehumanizing, capitalist healthcare system mired in patriarchy, white supremacy, ableism, and homophobia. The risk of harm to birthing people does not end with the birth of the baby. Mothers still have to navigate the challenges of early motherhood without proper structural support.

Long before I had babies, Motherhood's PR team convinced me that "breast is best." During both pregnancies, I squeezed my nipples in the shower until I expressed a cloudy drop. "I have milk!" I shrieked to Paul. After delivering Ollie, the hospital staff assumed I would breastfeed. The nurses listed off the benefits but didn't provide me with the resources I needed to be successful once I was at home.

Newborn Ollie nursed constantly. I was having terrible nipple pain, but I didn't want to deny my baby, so I continued anyway. After nursing, he'd last maybe twenty minutes before his crying would start up again.

"I think he's hungry," Paul would say.

"He can't be hungry. I *just* nursed him."

"I'm going to make him a bottle of formula."

"No! Don't," I'd say, my hand a stop sign. *I can meet all his needs. It has to be me.*

"I'll just make him a bottle, and if he isn't hungry, he won't drink it," Paul would respond, always the reasonable one, while I'd have punishing thoughts like, *I should be able to do this.* Without proper structural support, "the best job a woman can have" becomes an experience to "get through." *Just grin and bear it.*

"Fine," I'd agree, tears streaming down my face, unsure why I felt so much pressure for all of Ollie's nutrients to come from my body, even when it hurt. "Let me feed him, though."

To Paul's credit, he didn't shame or deny me. Instead, he laid Ollie on my lap and handed me the bottle, without a word. Ollie filled up the silence with his slurping until he'd gulped down every last drop.

The pain I felt with nursing got bad enough that after four weeks I flipped my care source from "Mommy" to "Money," and shelled out a couple hundred dollars for a lactation consultant to come to our home. She showed me that Ollie wasn't latching correctly, which is why it hurt so badly. Without a proper latch, Ollie wasn't getting enough milk. My baby really was hungry.

Babies are hospitalized and die because of this same scenario. If I'd been getting proper postpartum care, I wouldn't have waited so long to attend to my own pain because someone would have been checking on me. And I wouldn't have had to pay out of pocket for nursing support, a luxury many parents don't have. Mom support groups, lactation consultants, midwives, doulas, mental health professionals, pelvic floor therapists—none of these care resources are guaranteed for American mothers. Instead, these postpartum necessities are treated like fringe benefits.

Damp and sour-smelling, alternating between blissed-out and bereft, and possibly bleeding and still waddling (one mom I interviewed described her vagina tearing in the shape of a *spiral*), American moms are told they are "good to go" at the six-week postpartum doctor appointment. It varies by state, but federal law only requires states to extend pregnancy-related eligibility for Medicaid and CHIP (Children's Health Insurance Program) until sixty days postpartum. This is important because these programs cover almost half of all births nationally. The six-week appointment marks the moment that the support faucet, already barely dripping, completely shuts off. The system dries its washed hands satisfactorily—*All done! No more care needed!*—despite 12 percent of all maternal deaths taking place *after* the six-week postpartum mark.

Though I had round-the-clock encouragement from hospital staff to nurse my babies, I received no information, no warning, not even a mention of what could happen to me when I *stopped* nursing. After eight glorious months of feeling like a milky fembot goddess, spraying milk across the room if Ollie popped off my nipple while nursing, my supply began to dwindle.

My rage and my milk supply seemed to be inversely related. As my milk went down, my rage began in earnest. My breast milk disappeared completely by Ollie's first birthday, and soon my periods returned with an unfamiliar ferocity. My body was going through a major hormonal shift, and I felt wrecked for half of every month. I can best describe my emotional experience as sharp irritation that exploded often and uncontrollably.

Paul told me in no uncertain terms I needed to get help. My primary care doctor diagnosed me with PMDD (premenstrual dysphoric disorder), one of those "women's diagnoses" no one seems to quite understand, which results in a lot of guesswork and inadequate care. The doctor started me on Prozac. Over the next couple of years, I tried low doses of a few different antidepressants and antianxiety medications. I tried taking them for the ten days before my period, but my periods have always been irregular and I could never keep track. I tried taking the medications every day. Did they work? I don't know. I still had mom rage, and neither the circumstances in my home nor the neglectful structures that impacted my home had changed.

The deficiencies in mothercare don't stop at medical care, education, and access to expertise. America also refuses to guarantee new parents the valuable resource of time—time for the family to bond, time to ease into new daily rhythms, time for the mother's body to heal. In 2019, UNICEF ranked forty-one middle- and high-income countries based on four factors. Two of those factors were paid maternity leave and paid paternity leave. The US ranked last in both.

Without paid family leave for both parents, it is exceptionally difficult for mothers and birthing people to access help. Ceci, a Mexican American paralegal I interviewed, experienced this following the birth of her son. She and her husband had moved temporarily from Southern California to the San Francisco Bay Area, where she gave birth. At one of her son's initial pediatrician appointments, Ceci was given the "How are you feeling?" checklist that is supposed to catch postpartum mood and anxiety disorders like postpartum depression, postpartum anxiety, and postpartum psychosis. Based on her responses, she was referred to a therapist. But after an initial intake, Ceci never returned.

Ceci wasn't being defiant by not going to therapy—she was being pragmatic. "You know how everything is over there. Finding parking is a nightmare. Carrying the baby in his car seat is so heavy. It was just too daunting." Having someone else watch the baby during her appointments would have made all this much easier. But there was no one. The week she gave birth was the one week her husband took off from work. Ceci isn't sure if he could have asked for paternity leave from his job. "He was working at a law firm owned by three boomer-generation men, [all of whom] had wives who stayed home. It wasn't really a 'thing' to take time off as a dad." Here is yet another way the culture funnels mothers into the role of primary parent. The absence of a federal leave policy for partners is structural discrimination for multiple reasons, including that it denies birthing people the postpartum help of their partners.

Fewer than 5 percent of fathers take at least two weeks of paternity leave in the US. This is understandable when patriarchal corporate work culture makes dads fear that if they take their entire paternity leave, it might hurt their professional futures. Due to cultural expectations on fathers to "bring home the bacon," and the structural inequalities (gender pay gap, fatherhood bonus) that often make dads' jobs better compensated than their wives', fathers tend to carry the bulk of a family's financial responsibilities. Because of this fiscal burden, if a father's job has a paternity leave policy that is unpaid or only pays at a percentage of his salary, he is less likely to be able to take his full leave without exchanging stability for precarity.

In the first two weeks after the birth, Ceci had help from her husband, her mother, and her mother-in-law. In her third week postpartum, still healing from an unplanned C-section and struggling with gastrointestinal problems and nursing issues (blisters, cracked nipples, the whole painful shebang), Ceci was all alone, the sole caregiver of her baby.

"In Mexican culture, women are really taken care of after they have babies, at least for forty days," Ceci explained. She was referring to *la cuarentena*, a postpartum tradition in many Latin American cultures, from Guatemala to Mexico to the Dominican Republic, in which the new mother stays home to rest for forty days. A key idea of *la cuarentena* is "closing the body," which is believed to be open after birth. Traditionally the new mother keeps her head covered and keeps her abdomen tightly wrapped in fabric. She is supposed to eat certain foods (chicken soup) and avoid others (spicy foods).

Similar to *la cuarentena* is the thirty-day Chinese postpartum tradition of *zuo yue zi*, which translates to "confinement." In English it is usually called "sitting the month." The practice is meant to keep a mother healthy in the long and short term by balancing her energy after the blood loss that happens in childbirth, which the Chinese believe can put a mother in an out-of-balanced state of yin (cold). During *zuo yue zi*, moms are supposed to avoid cold things, like ice water and air conditioning. They are encouraged to eat certain foods to improve health, like warm pigs' feet soup, which has necessary nutrients and contains yang energy. Traditionally, sitting the month also includes wrapping a long piece of cloth around the mom's stomach.

La cuarentena and *zuo yue zi* are considered special times when the mother and baby stay home together and bond while their community, which is usually women like the mother's mother and mother-in-law, does the housework, cooks, and cares for the new mother and any older children. The specifics of both rituals vary from country to country, and from mother to mother. Mothers who are intimately familiar with either tradition warn that they can be done to the extreme, and not every rule makes sense.

"So, did you do *la cuarentena*?" I asked Ceci. Though she identifies as mestiza and her roots are in Mexico, Ceci's life is in America, where there are no postpartum rituals for new mothers and minimal structural support.

"No. I took my son out within two weeks. I had to go have some wine and oysters!" Ceci laughed. Then in the same breath she added, "I didn't have anybody. No one was going to take care of me." Not her family, and not the state. Ceci did end up having (untreated) postpartum depression and mom rage. When she was finally able to get herself some support and go to therapy, it wasn't until four years later.

Zaara, the mom who fostered and adopted her two daughters in Minneapolis, was able to get therapy when her rage became a problem. She credits therapy with helping her realize that her rage is really at the system and its neglect of communities and families. With her background in equity and education, Zaara was keenly aware of how the deck is stacked against foster kids and the harrowing statistics about their future, like only 4 percent of foster kids graduate from college. "When I was raging, I wasn't really reacting to an eight-year-old who doesn't feel like doing math because it's boring. I was reacting to 'Oh my god, you're going to be homeless because you're not going to finish college.'"

Zaara's rage was at its height during the rise of Black Lives Matter, when police brutality against Black people was on national news nightly. It's well documented that repetitively experiencing racial discrimination increases a person's risk for chronic stress, and can result in depression, anxiety, and other psychological disorders. As a South Asian woman who grew up wearing a hijab in Tennessee—a state with a non-Hispanic white population of 73 percent—Zaara is familiar with race-related stress. But as a new mother to Black girls, her stress, fear, and rage skyrocketed. She was afraid, particularly for one of her daughters who has PTSD, which makes her "react huge to small things." When the kids would touch the gum at a grocery store, Zaara would angrily scream, "Don't touch that!" But Zaara said that underneath this reaction was a deep fear: "If you touch that they're going to assume you stole it, you're gonna be arrested, the police are going to kill you."

Zaara adores her daughters and is so glad they came into her life. At the same time, she is angry about the many layers of systemic neglect that brought them to her. She said her daughters' biological family wasn't "bad"; they were underresourced and faced "everything that comes with living in a low-income area, like generations of drug abuse and community disinvestment, and what that can do to a single mother." Zaara is mad that after her daughters were taken from their biological mother, they were traumatized in a system meant to protect them. She added, "That same system paid me X amount of money every month but didn't provide mental health care to their biological mom! There was just so much rage."

The labor of mothering is more than trips to the playground, more than making dinner or reminding an older kid to "please see to those toenails." It's making sure kids know who to trust, how to speak to authority figures, and what to do in an emergency.

Mothering is the eternal sketching of protection maps, seeing the structural pitfalls seven steps ahead, and weaving nets, always ready to catch. Because so much of the work of caring for children falls on mothers, we are the ones most heavily impacted by the failures of social systems meant to protect and take care of children.

The 2019 UNICEF study that ranked forty-one middle- and high-income nations on maternity and paternity leave also ranked on two other factors: state childcare for kids under three and state childcare for kids between three and school age. Again, the US came in last place. When a society pushes mothers into the role of primary parent and then refuses to provide adequate care for the children, mothers are forced to sacrifice everything else in their lives to step in where the society has stepped out.

For six and a half years most of my days were spent doing childcare. Even when Ollie was in private childcare, which we were privileged enough to be able to afford, it was morning-only programs that seemed to best meet his needs. This meant that on top of nursing Mae throughout the night and taking care of both kids from six to nine in the morning, I was also doing childcare from twelve thirty in the afternoon till bedtime. Paul and I were grinding so hard, stuck in what felt like an endless loop of working and childcare, that we barely realized it when something miraculous happened—we made it to the promised land: public school.

On a warm August evening in 2019, Paul and I filed into Ollie's first grade classroom with thirty or so other parents for back-to-school night. It's a parenting rite of passage to experience the singular indignity of using one's grown-up-sized behind to test the weight limit of tiny plastic school chairs. With hunched shoulders, we made ourselves small, nodding as Ollie's teacher went over her plan for the year. She segued into how eager she was to work with that year's room parent. At Ollie's school, room parents act as the liaison between the parents and teacher. They help out in the classroom, send out weekly emails, organize events, and set up online wish lists for classroom needs like paper towels or books. Ollie's bright-eyed teacher looked out at the sea of eager parents.

"Are there any volunteers?"

I was nervous for Ollie. This was his first time in a full day of school. For kindergarten the year before, he'd attended a "forest school," an outdoor learning environment that uses the natural surroundings for personal, social, and academic growth, and had flourished from all the flexibility and space it provided a neurodivergent child. If circle time was too much sensory input, Ollie was allowed to climb a tree and listen from the safe distance of a hovering limb. I feared that traditional public school would be more rigid, and as a result, his needs might get misconstrued as behavior problems. I'd been by Ollie's side for years, conferencing almost daily with his teachers at pickup and drop-off, a staunch advocate for his needs. Now I was just going to put Ollie on a school bus and wave, fingers crossed that he'd learn and be seen and cared for until the bus came back seven hours later? It felt like a wild leap of faith.

So when Ollie's teacher asked for a volunteer room parent, my tentative hand began to lift from my lap. Paul spied its trajectory. His own hand darted out and pressed mine back down in the nick of time.

"What are you doing?" he whisper-hissed. I sort of shrugged, not able to explain in that moment my concerns about Ollie thriving at public school. Instead, I motioned to all the other volunteering mothers (there was not a single father with a raised hand in that room), as if to say, *Look around. This is what (good) mothers do. Plus,* I thought, *Ollie might need me.*

"You do *not* want to be the room parent," Paul said pointedly. The intensity of his look reflected my years of rage—how angry I'd been at Ollie's preschools for not being able to give him the care he needed, and how resentful I was that when the system failed Ollie, *I* was the fallback answer, my career be damned. I knew Paul was right. With two-year-old Mae in all-day preschool, this was the first time since becoming a mother that I'd have almost a full day to write. I'd worked so hard to get to this turning point, but . . .

"He'll be fine," Paul insisted, seeing my love (disguised as worry) swim around my face.

My inclination to be a room parent because I felt my child might need an advocate in a system that isn't built for him is not unique. In the few years since that day, Ollie has had two room parents, both of whom now hold positions on the school's parent teacher association. (Apparently, room parent is a gateway position to the PTA.) One of the former room parents works tirelessly to ensure children with disabilities have equal access to the same education as everyone else. Like Ollie, her son has an IEP (individualized education program) to support his special needs. The other is working to create an Asian American and Pacific Islander taskforce to get district-wide protocols in place for handling racist comments. Her children are Asian American.

In essence, room parents and PTA members are doing their best to advocate for their children. My kids' school district is fairly mixed racially (41 percent of students are white) and somewhat mixed economically (30 percent of students receive free or reduced-price meals at school), and it is in a heavily Democratic-leaning city. Despite this, parents feel they must step into active roles at their kids' schools to strong-arm a racist, ableist, classist, homophobic system into taking care of their most precious people. These mothers are fighting systemic injustice on behalf of their children, sometimes putting their own physical bodies in the way. I imagined that if I were a room parent, I could step in if the teacher was being cross with Ollie for not paying attention. I could make sure he is getting the supports he is entitled to during a test, as stated in his IEP. I could protect him.

My anxiety—a direct throughline to my rage—isn't exceptional; it's an expected part of being one of the 25 percent of homes in the US that have a child with special healthcare needs and have to fight for those kids in a system that wasn't designed for their success. In a 2009 study conducted by Leann Smith and colleagues, moms of kids on the autism spectrum reported spending at least two more hours a day on caregiving than moms of kids without disabilities. They were also "twice as likely to be tired and three times as likely to have experienced a stressful event." Anxiety, frustration, rage—these are the results of stressed-out mothers who are working extremely hard to both get through the day and support their children in a system that doesn't.

Parenting kids with special needs exacerbates mom rage, not because the kids' behaviors are rage inducing—though, lord help me, sometimes they are—but because of the energy, frustration, and time it takes to get these kids the support and care they need. From ages four to six, getting Ollie properly supported was a full-time job: assessments for sensory processing disorder and then autism spectrum disorder, a school IEP, occupational therapy for fine and gross motor delays and food rigidity, social skills groups for kids on the autism spectrum, multiple behaviorists, a one-on-one aide, meetings with teachers, and the never-ending phone calls with health insurance to get them to cover the costs. If mothers want their children to have the education and medical care they need and deserve, we are forced to sacrifice our time, energy, and sometimes our mental wellness.

This labor—including being a room parent and joining the PTA—can't be considered voluntary if the society won't offer another solution, and our children and families suffer without it. A 2020 report by the Century Foundation said that US schools are underfunded by $150 billion a year. Funding disparities are deepest in districts with majority Black, Latinx, and low-income families. Some PTAs raise money for a variety of needs that many school districts can't pay for, like after-school programs, gardening classes, physical education teachers, field trips, art teachers, musical instruments, and gift cards for families with financial struggles. With schools being greatly underfunded, the "voluntary" labor of the (mostly) mother-run PTA has become an integral system that families, educators, school districts, governments, and the entire society have come to depend on.

The PTA is considered voluntary because it's unpaid. It's unpaid because of the feminization and racialization of care work. Care work is the work done to take care of others, including childcare, teaching, laundry, housework, care for elderly, sick, and disabled people, and other invisible labor. Care work is often not seen as work because of the assumption it's being performed purely out of love—the very same love that's co-opted by Motherhood's PR campaign. During industrialization, care work became women's work, and it was racialized during slavery, when white people forced Black women to do the housework and childcare.

This history is present today in the continued exploitation of unpaid mothers and underpaid care workers. The median annual salary for early childhood educators in the US in 2021 was $27,680, which is barely above the federal poverty level for a family of four in 2021 ($26,500). The early childhood education sector is made up of 95 percent women. Domestic workers (nannies, housecleaners, and in-home care aides for children, the elderly, sick, and disabled) are 91.5 percent women, predominantly women of color and immigrants. Underpaying or not paying for someone's time and expertise doesn't necessarily mean the labor is voluntary, but it does reveal how little the labor, and the people doing the labor, are valued and cared for by the society.

Though I have not taken on roles at my kids' schools, I wanted to interview a mom who did. Cassandra is a married, working-class, Caribbean-born Black mother, whose three kids were at Title I schools in Brooklyn, New York, until her youngest graduated high school in 2021. Title I provides federal money to public schools with a high number of students from low-income families. Low-income school districts in the US are twice as likely to experience a funding gap as higher-income districts, with an average gap of $6,700 per student. It was important to Cassandra to have a say in how the Title I money got spent at her children's schools. "The school principal has to give a budgetary report. Parents can ask questions. We have a voice," she explained. "That, for me, was everything. For inner city schools, [being involved in the school] allows you to feel more in control of your kids' lives."

Cassandra was on the PTA for her children's schools from preschool all the way through high school. She estimates that the many PTAs she was a part of were all composed of 98 percent mothers. The unpaid labor of room mother (let's just call it what it is, shall we?) and the PTA are merely extensions of the modern-day job description of Mother. Like the two room mothers in Ollie's classrooms, Cassandra was stepping in to ensure her children, and by extension all the children at the school, were being properly taken care of—mothered—in a system that values cost-saving over care.

Today's parents with paid jobs (which is most parents) don't have time for the PTA. But moms are expected to *make* time. Cassandra worked at the airport in the afternoons and evenings, sometimes getting off as late as one in the morning. This schedule allowed her (at the cost of sleep hours) to do the work that she says "needed doing" at her kids' schools during the first part of the day. Cassandra averaged twenty hours a month doing work for her children's schools. Even with summers off, that's two hundred hours of work per year that benefits a system that refuses to acknowledge such labor as real work or financially compensate it. This society-wide refusal positions mothers' stress and anger into a place of seeming illegitimacy. (*Why are you complaining? It's voluntary.*)

Poor and nonexistent structural care is felt even more acutely in the summer. The fallout, once again, is on moms. "When I was raising my kids, I was always thinking, 'What's next to do?' When January come, I gotta think of summer camp. I gotta get their medicals in February or March, so they'll be ready for camp or the next grade," said Cassandra, who described March as one of her "broke months." It was when her car insurance payment was due. "Even with my tax return, I had to start planning for the summertime around then, putting down payments, because not every camp is going to be free."

According to the American Camp Association, the average *daily* cost for day camp in 2022 is $178. It's $449 for overnight camp. Multiply that to get the cost of a ten-week summer! And that's just for one child. The high price of summer camp turns a childcare necessity into an extravagance for the wealthy. A study from the US Department of Education shows that only 7 percent of kids from poor families have access to summer programming. And while there are scholarships as well as low-cost and even free options, the lack of access reverberates throughout society. Without summer programming to fill the gap, the summer months result in learning loss that drives half of the achievement gap between affluent and lower-income students. In her newsletter *Culture Study*, Anne Helen Petersen writes, "Essentially, we treat all the care that kids need and get outside of school hours as a private good, not a public one. . . . When we treat public goods as private goods, we create markets that are ripe for inequality. Because the cost to provide those goods far outpaces what most people who need those goods can afford."

In early spring, Cassandra, like every other primary parent, rich or poor, who isn't able to stay home for ten weeks, is tasked with the invisible labor of researching, scheduling, and booking a summer's worth of childcare. Never mind that 80 percent of mothers with children under age eighteen work full-time paid jobs. If they don't do the annual summertime care scramble, the responsibility of watching children all day every day for ten long weeks will fall to them. How convenient for society to view summer camp as optional when the alternative is mom.

With no structural care system in America—just "Money or Mommy"—it quickly becomes a very real possibility that *no one* will be able to watch the kids, which is disproportionately likely for low-income families and children of color. Despite this inevitable outcome of making summer camp a private good, guess who will be the one to get side-eye or worse when something goes wrong? Here's a clue: it will not be the father.

Before parents can even graduate to the summer camp quandary or the dilemma of what to do with their children every day after school before the workday ends, they must first survive the Hunger Games–style bloodbath that is patching together childcare for the first five years of each child's life. That is, if it even makes financial sense to pay for daycare and preschool, the cost of which tripled between 1990 and 2020, then increased by 41 percent during the pandemic while wages have not kept pace with these increases in costs. When childcare costs more than parents make, mothers are the fallback. Moms are approximately three times more likely than fathers to quit a job for caregiving reasons.

The childcare problem, which is also a mothercare problem, is not inevitable. The US *chooses* not to spend money on childcare because we don't see it as societal infrastructure. But we could! Other countries do. The average amount that other rich countries spend annually on childcare breaks down to $14,436 per child. Coincidentally (or not), $14,000 is the amount the average American family living in a major metropolis spends on childcare per year. But instead of creating structural support for families, the US lets the anvil of privatized childcare rest on the shoulders of each individual family. If we add up the minimal subsidies and early childhood education programs the government *does* fund, the US spends a whopping $500 a year per kid. This meager funding is beyond insufficient and results in inequities, like one in three American children beginning kindergarten without having had any preschool at all. By refusing to create care structures, the US is *choosing* to drop the burden directly into mothers' laps.

Mothers *are* America's care infrastructure, and it's costing us emotionally. Though there aren't many studies measuring mothers' anger, we do measure postpartum depression, of which anger can be a symptom. Prepandemic, the (reported) rate of birthing people in the US with postpartum depression was 15 to 20 percent. During the summer of 2020, the rates were reported to be 36 percent. A key determinant for both mom rage and postpartum depression is a lack of support. With no childcare that summer, moms acutely felt the burden of America's "Money or Mommy" care system.

We can't blame the slide of mothers' mental wellness completely on the pandemic. Schools reopened in the fall of 2021. But by winter, groups of mothers were reported to be gathering in fields in cities across the US to scream together. In the house or in a field, screaming is the current emotional state of motherhood.

And while the pandemic may have pushed mothers over the edge, we've been teetering there as unsupported caregivers for decades.

It costs mothers professionally to fill in for the state's choice not to fund universal daycare, preschool, after-school care, and summer camp. It affects the types of jobs moms take and how much they can work. Almost half of American mothers "voluntarily" reduce their hours to care for a family member, compared to 28 percent of fathers. This includes not only childcare, but also eldercare. Of the 40 million people caring for their parents and grandparents, 8.2 million also have a child under the age of eighteen at home. Burdened with the responsibility of caring for the generations before and after them, these mostly female caregivers are sometimes called "the sandwich generation."

Forty-one-year-old Eloise is a member of the sandwich generation. Eloise is Kalmyk Mongol American; she said her mom was the very first of their ethnic group born in the US. The weight of caregiving falls heaviest on mothers from low-income and immigrant families, like the one Eloise grew up in. As a child and young adult, Eloise watched her own mother take care of most of her family, navigating a wide range of loved ones' health issues, from addiction to diabetes to cancer to schizophrenia. Now, at sixty-nine, Eloise's mother has a slew of her own health issues, including rheumatoid arthritis, breathing problems from COPD, and depression. She takes nineteen different medications and was hospitalized twice in the last year. Eloise attends all her mom's health appointments and tries to make sure her mother, who lives independently, is not alone too often. Eloise's long-term plan is to have her mom come live with her.

When we spoke, Eloise's house was pretty full. She and her husband live in Philadelphia with their two children, ages nine and twelve. For the last five years, Eloise's father-in-law, also sixty-nine, has been living with them. He has bipolar schizoaffective disorder. Though he is stable, he needs the family to take him to his doctor's appointments, since he doesn't drive. As all parents know, caregiving is both the big things, like being there for hours in the hospital when problems arise, and the small everyday things, like Eloise buying her father-in-law cigarettes and helping him use technology. On average, adults who live with the elder they take care of provide three hours a day of care. That's approximately ninety-one unpaid caregiving hours a month, or 1,095 hours a year. Those hours don't include the phone calls, research, and advocacy work that caring for someone requires. "It's not a small thing to navigate the social welfare system. It could be a full-time job," Eloise said, not mentioning that she already has a full-time job as a nonprofit strategist and consultant.

Here's how her care work correlates with her mom rage. Eloise, who is medicated for both depression and anxiety, said, "My mom rage is less severe now, in my forties, but I've definitely raged out and broken things. As a woman of color, who grew up working class and poor, my rage is partly around 'the system.'" Eloise wants the systems and individuals to do a better job of taking care of people. "People need to learn how to step up. It's not enough to be like, 'Oh, I offered help.' No! Go out of your way. That is how shit gets done."

A week after our interview Eloise made sure to protect (take care of) her husband by contacting me to ensure I understood that he does half the work in their household and for her mother. Yet having a helpful and engaged partner doesn't solve the systemic failure to take care of mothers. "Even with a partner who mostly steps up," Eloise added, "mom rage is still real."

Caregiving gets passed down, a heavy maternal lineage. At the end of our interview, Eloise reflected, "I grew up with my mother always taking care of somebody. I don't want that to be what my kids think of with me." But what choice does Eloise have? Mothers and the government are in a perverse game of chicken—who will budge first and take care of the people? If we can't afford quality care for our loved ones, we either have to put them in suboptimal situations or we have to do it ourselves for free.

Of course, free isn't actually free, just as the PTA isn't really voluntary and summer camp isn't truly optional. Mothers' care work is currently unpaid, but it's not worthless. In 2019, Oxfam estimated that if the 12.5 billion hours of unpaid care work done around the world were compensated at minimum wage, it would be worth almost $11 trillion—three times the worth of the global tech industry.

Patti Maciesz is a mother artist and creator of Bill the Patriarchy, a website where caregivers can enter the amount of time they spend doing care work, give themselves an hourly wage, and see what their annual salary would be if they were paid for their labor. Maciesz told me she does eight hours of childcare a day (from five until nine in the morning, and again from five until nine at night) when her two kids, a two-year-old and five-year-old, are in full-time care. During the pandemic, she said it doubled and was more like eighteen hours with night wakings. An eighteen-hour workday is a 126-hour workweek. That's more than three full-time jobs, and there are no weekends off.

Maciesz reports that of the five thousand people who have participated in Bill the Patriarchy, most give themselves an hourly wage of twenty dollars or less. Still, the average annual salary on the site is $160,000, demonstrating just how much time is spent on unpaid care work, and what that labor would be worth if it were compensated.

Mothers' labor culturally and financially sustains our society. In return, society denies mothers the care we need to live happy, healthy, fully actualized lives. We create and birth the world's children while being treated by a medical system that doesn't understand our bodies and doesn't care to, resulting in America being the most dangerous developed nation to become a mother. Postpartum care amounts to being told to grin and bear it, which is good practice for the rest of our (caregiving) lives. With no care infrastructure other than "Money or Mommy," mothers are left with no choice but to do the childcare, mothercare, and eldercare ourselves. We hold down multiple jobs, paid and unpaid, and work ourselves into a perma-state of exhaustion, resentment, and, inevitably, rage.

When we think about how the PR team convinces us to become mothers, then add up the myriad ways society neglects to take proper care of us and our loved ones while profiting from our coerced, unpaid labor, it is easy to see how mom rage is an expression of despair. But here's the thing about rage: it is an acknowledgment that there is a problem. If moms are slamming doors and throwing produce across the room, then we've stopped performing maternal bliss. By raging, we're calling bullshit on the scam of Motherhood.

"Rage is a kind of refusal," writes Brittney Cooper, author and professor of women's and gender studies. Most moms have little or no choice but to navigate the existing systems, damaging and paltry as they are. But when we rage, we signal our refusal to be mistreated, undervalued, and uncared for. Without this first fueling step of anger, there will be no change in the family structure or the societal systems. Mothers need that change, and I'm going to explore how we can get it. But first, can we give ourselves a minute to sit in the blistering heat of our anger? Rage need not be productive to be valid. In a culture that worships productivity but doesn't take care of mothers, it is a revolutionary act of self-care for mothers to allow ourselves to just be mad. If *we* don't give our fury space to exist, who will?

4 MATRESCENCE AND THE GASLIGHTING OF MOTHERS

> Her sense that society, adulthood, marriage, motherhood, all these things, were somehow masterfully designed to put a woman in her place and keep her there—this idea had begun to weigh on her. . . . And once she was stripped of all she had been, of her career, her comely figure, her ambition, her familiar hormones, an anti-feminist conspiracy seemed not only plausible but nearly inevitable.
>
> —Rachel Yoder, *Nightbitch*

The journey into motherhood begins with the body.

Regardless of whether the mother births the baby, or the baby is adopted, fostered, or born via surrogate, or whether the mother breastfeeds, chestfeeds, or bottle-feeds, the mother's body changes. Her new body is for rocking and comforting, wiping crevices clean, pushing marshmallow arms through sleeve tunnels, and giving gentle, baby caresses. Later, the mother's body will be for restraining her newly wiggly and non-compliant child so she can get his diaper or seatbelt on, for hugging the tantruming child (or digging her nails into her palms as she waits the tantrum out), for firmly holding wrists when the child hits her repeatedly, for running faster than she has ever run with arms outstretched to reach the child before he swan-dives into the street. Her body is a catchall for her child's body and emotions all day every day. Long after birth, the mother remains a container.

As a mother's body morphs in its physique and range of purpose, so do most other aspects of her life. A mother doesn't just have a new baby, she has a new life. She spins on a new axis. What used to be "day" and "night" bleed into each other until there is just a ticking clock with a smattering of numbers playing musical chairs. She has a new job, a sharp learning curve, a changing set of priorities, a shifting relationship dynamic (if she's partnered), and an altered sense of her value in the world.

A mother is so enmeshed with her child as she shimmies her way into her new identity that she often loses sight of her previous one, her former complexities fading until she is "just mother."

I overhear a pregnant woman say to her friend, "I don't want to lose myself once I become a mother." *What self?* I think as I pass her by. *She is already gone.*

Even her name begins to disappear . . .

———

It is 2013, and I am pointing out the yellow fish swimming in the tank to three-week-old Ollie, watching his eyes to see if he can focus on it.

"Mom, do you have his immunizations? Mom? *Mom?*"

I turn, startled. The receptionist at the pediatrician's office is standing behind the desk, reaching her hand out through the hole in the glass partition, looking at me expectantly.

"Oh!" I laugh and press my hand to the place my chest should be, which instead is Ollie, snug against me in a baby wrap. "You're talking to *me*?"

Why is she calling me Mom? I wonder. *My name is in the computer, isn't it? On all the documents?* I remember the hospital personnel calling me Mom after I gave birth to Ollie. It felt warranted then, an honorific that properly acknowledged pregnancy and birth, and my transition to the other side—the motherside. But now, out in the world, away from the miracle and carnage of the birthing room, it sounds strange.

I will experience this over and over. When I am in public with my kids, my name ceases to matter. Strangers everywhere—at my kids' schools, the playground, the bus, the YMCA—call me Mom. I wonder why people feel they have access to a name that belongs in my children's mouths. It's as if the world is relieved I am finally something capturable.

Pre-motherhood I was slippery, a thousand tiny, silver fish—a woman, a writer, a friend, an educator, a queer person, a performer, a Philly girl, a Bay Area transplant, a wife, a lefty Jew. With nothing to lose, no property, no fancy job, no kids, I was a flight risk. I could do or say anything. But now that I have children, I can't stray too far, mouth off too much. There are children to consider! To feed. To pick up from school. Mothers have obligations, schedules, other people to put first. My name has been erased, and I'm reduced to one role, one thing. As a mother, I am palatable, contained, tethered. People know how to categorize my mother-self.

"I'm Minna," I say, smiling at the receptionist like our mutual friend just introduced us, as I give her Ollie's immunization forms. Then I put out my hand to shake hers. She places her cool limp hand in mine, searching my eyes for hints of madness. *I'm trying not to lose my very self*, my eyes reply. She pulls her hand back carefully.

"The doctor will be right with you."

———

The transition into motherhood is called *matrescence*. The term was coined in the 1970s by Dana Raphael, a medical anthropologist, author, and breastfeeding advocate who also popularized the term *doula*. It is no coincidence matrescence sounds like adolescence. Both adolescence (the process of becoming an adult) and matrescence (the process of becoming a mother) are all-encompassing life phases that result in physical, social, cultural, psychological, and neurological changes.

Spanish neuroscientist Susanna Carmona studies the pregnancy and postpartum brain. In a study published in 2019, she and her team used MRI to compare the brains of twenty-five mothers during and after pregnancy, twenty-five girls pre- and post-adolescence, and a control group of women who'd never been pregnant. Carmona found that the structural brain changes observed in adolescents, which include gray matter reduction and decreases in cortical thickness and surface area, were identical to the brain changes found in mothers.

On the podcast *Mommy Brain Revisited*, Carmona described her results to host Jodi Pawluski, who studies the neuroscience of motherhood: "Both [adolescence and matrescence] are transitional life periods that entail a series of behavioral changes to face the challenges ahead. And also a change in self-perception. They are also characterized by abrupt increases in sex hormones. And now, with this [study], we also show that both entail similar neuroanatomical adaptations."

More research needs to be funded and conducted to fully understand the functional effects of these structural brain changes. But a 2017 study, co-led by Carmona and her colleague, neuroscientist Óscar Vilarroya, found that the structural brain changes are likely part of a neurological process called *synaptic pruning*, a fine-tuning of the brain that aids us in letting go of information we no longer need to remember, like a character's name in a book. Some theorize that synaptic pruning could be the neurological explanation for the matrescence phenomenon known as "mom brain," when new mothers make silly mistakes and forget things (like their keys in the locked car), and generally feel like their brains aren't working at full capacity. (Another likely cause of mom brain: sleep-deprived mothers being responsible for the health and well-being of multiple people while transforming into new selves without adequate support from partners or society.)

The natural shedding that occurs with synaptic pruning allows our brains to make room for new information that will help us better accomplish the tasks required in an upcoming life phase. For example, in adolescence, a reduction in cortical thickness and gray matter correlates with better executive function for things like time management and task completion, which adulthood requires. The same neurological changes aid new mothers in forming attachment bonds to their babies. Using fMRI, Carmona and her team observed that the greater the reduction in a mother's gray matter, the more her brain responds to pictures of her baby. We know these brain changes stick around for at least two years postpartum, possibly longer. More research of the maternal brain could tell us if the neurological adaptations of matrescence are permanent.

Aurélie Athan, reproductive psychologist and head of the Maternal & Reproductive Psychology Laboratory at Teachers College at Columbia University, who revived the term *matrescence* from its

1970s origins through her research and teaching, says that "the exact length of matrescence is individual, recurs with each child, and may arguably last a lifetime." For some, matrescence might begin once the child is born. For others it could commence during pregnancy or even before, while freezing eggs, applying to adopt or foster, or taking hormones for IVF. And with each new phase of childhood, we enter a new stage of motherhood. The process of becoming our mother-selves never really stops.

Yet societal support for people transitioning into motherhood is minimal, and what is available is purely medical. A birthing person might get a perineum tear stitched up immediately after birth, but no one is following up about how her inability to walk for the next three months impacts her mental wellness during her entrée into matrescence. "We have conversations and normalizing and support around [adolescence]," says reproductive psychiatrist Alexandra Sacks, who popularized the term *matrescence* through articles in the *New York Times* and *Psychology Today*. But we have none of these, says Sacks, for "the analogous transition that happens to a woman when she becomes a mother."

In the US, many communities have coming-of-age rituals that honor adolescents' entrance into their new life phase: the Amish *rumspringa*; the Latin American *quinceañeras*; the debutante balls of the American South; the bar and bat mitzvahs for Jewish youth; the Apache Sunrise Ceremony; and the ballgown-and-tiara sweet sixteen parties. Even American teens without a particular coming-of-age ritual learn from each other and engage in communal identity-building by being together in middle and high school, on the basketball court, or at church or summer camp, often for more hours a day than they are with their families.

Matrescence, on the other hand, is worked through mostly in the isolation of our homes. Our new mother-selves are rarely acknowledged, let alone celebrated. Baby showers, the closest we have to an American motherhood ritual, focus on the soon-to-arrive baby, not the arrival of the mother. Mothers themselves are swept along in this baby-centered tidal wave. It can take months, sometimes years, for mothers to realize they've been devoting every ounce of their energy to the needs of the baby, their own needs barely detectable anymore.

Through her research and teaching on matrescence, Athan works to create "a missing model of psychological development for the emerging mother." A society that honors matrescence would empower and support all kinds of mothers to "identify, explore, cope with, and shape their destinies according to their own individual differences. This same gift was once given to adolescents who before they were named as such were merely thought to be children going mad on the way to adulthood."

I can't help but make the comparison with mom rage. When adolescence was acknowledged as a metamorphic life phase at the turn of the twentieth century, it completely changed the way we care for and understand our teenagers. Without the same research, recognition, and support that is dedicated to adolescence, matrescence and the fury that so often accompanies it can easily be written off as "moms going mad."

When we become our new mother-selves, we struggle to hold onto parts of our old selves. Athan describes matrescence as "an experience of dis-orientation and re-orientation." But what mother can process either one when the daily goal is survival?

After becoming a mom, Lauren, the Anglo-Australian with the British travel agent husband she described as "a bit of a grown-up boy," struggled to get back into the arts scene in Perth, Australia: "I lost confidence in myself as a person in the world with my own identity, desires, and ambitions." While managing the disorientation of having lost connection to pieces of her old self, Lauren worked to integrate the new roles she'd taken on in the home:

"mediator, counselor, carer, domestic worker, and family-unity manager." She said, "Here I was, doing the most demanding, sophisticated, interpersonal work that had an impact on the lives of several people." Yet, instead of feeling powerful, Lauren felt like she was shrinking into "just a mum."

Despite her "joyous, warm, and loving" relationship with her son, Lauren felt constricted by the social role of Mother. "It feels like an oppressive container, almost like a costume. But I don't suddenly want to wear florals and bake cupcakes and be pious about my child's every move. I still want to swear and drink a pint of beer. I'm still a sexual being. I'm interested in politics. I'm angry!"

Motherhood compressed Lauren's exquisite intricacies into a singular identity. She felt taken for granted and resentful of having to take care of everyone's physical and emotional needs before her own. Her resulting rage came out at her husband, but her true target was the power structures that built Motherhood and continue to benefit from it.

The invisibility of the deeply embedded oppression that is at the root of today's crisis of modern motherhood makes it easier for people to point at dissatisfied, raging mothers and pathologize them. The PR team tells us if a mom is angry about her circumstances or the life-altering, tectonic shift of matrescence—which is inextricably linked with the institutional and familial neglect of mothers—then *she* is the one who must be deranged or ill. When all fingers point to the mother, even she begins to turn her outstretched pointer finger back around to herself. Lauren admitted, "I sometimes end up thinking, 'It's me. I'm the mad woman.'" It *is* maddening to be living a version of motherhood that doesn't exist in the cultural narrative. Her experience is being denied everywhere she looks. This is how the culture gaslights mothers.

The gaslighting happens in large-scale systemic ways—*Why would mothers need institutional support or a break from "the best job a woman can have"?* It also happens in small everyday moments. Imagine an elderly lady clucking, "Aw, isn't it the best?" to a mom in the pharmacy line waiting to buy nipple cream and laxatives. The only socially appropriate response is a half-hearted exhalation followed by an affirmative "Heh, yeah," when actually it's not at all the best. But the mother can't say that because the stranger will stare at her, silently assessing, then glance at the baby with concern, because we must always protect the baby, never mind the mother. If a mother is insistent on voicing what is true—beyond the baby's skin being impossibly soft and her fuzzy head smelling like flour and honey—she runs the risk of being deemed deviant, negligent, or sick. Pressure to perform an external self that does not match her internal life creates a dissonance that's disorienting. It can sow doubt in a mother's psyche about whether her lived experience is valid and real.

I experienced this public shock and silent assessing when Ollie was five months old and I performed a monologue I wrote for an audience of a hundred people, including my in-laws. The piece is about the "four-month sleep regression," a time when a baby's brief stretches of nighttime sleep do the impossible—get even shorter. The piece also showcased my first moment of mom rage, though I didn't call it that back then.

On stage, I explained how Ollie's sleep had gone from two- and three-hour stretches to a mere sixty minutes. I told the audience that one night, after what felt like a thousand failed efforts of nursing and bouncing Ollie to sleep, I heard him cry out *again,* and I punched my mattress as hard as I could. Paul turned to me in bed and gently asked, "What do you need?" Quick like a light, I responded, "I need to not be his mother." When I said that, the entire audience gasped in unison. A heavy silence followed, and in those three seconds of dead air, I felt like I'd splintered a forbidden dimension with my unmotherly confession. What I'd done was publicly refuse to perform the culture's version of Mother.

Seven years later, reminiscing about that fifteen-minute performance that made the audience laugh and cry, my father-in-law told me that while he can recall thinking the entire performance was powerful, the only part he remembers is when I said, "I need to not be his mother."

"Why do you think that's the only line that stuck with you?" I asked, feigning innocence. My father-in-law looked up at the ceiling and let out a half-laugh, his palms face up.

"I'd never heard a mother say such a thing."

Loyal as ever, Paul said loudly from the next room, "It's a pretty common experience."

My father-in-law never heard a mother say such a thing because mothers aren't allowed to say it, even today, after all the progress of the first, second, and third waves of the feminist movement. Even after mom rage became a public talking point during the COVID-19 pandemic and was written about in articles from Israel to India, mothers are still navigating the always-looming risk of being deemed negligent, unfit, or unwell—all code for "bad mom." If a mother dares to speak up despite the cultural gaslighting, then she must decide if she is safe (privileged) enough to accept the other punishments for being honest about her rage. These may be as minimal as being judged or snubbed socially, or as risky as having one's children taken away. Poor moms, moms of color, moms in same-sex marriages, disabled moms, and immigrant moms are under increased risk and social pressure to deny their anger publicly and perform "good mother."

Every time I interviewed a mom for this book and asked her to tell me what her rage looks like, she would hesitate, and I would feel the weight of the risk. Thirty minutes into my video interview with Joelle, the British mother who had her baby at fifty-one with the help of IVF, I finally asked her the hardest question.

"Can you bring me into a rage moment, from buildup to explosion to aftermath?" Chatty and forthcoming for our whole interview, Joelle became quiet, then asked a question. Or maybe it was a declaration. I can't tell which.

"You're not going to take her away," she said. Goose bumps rose on my skin. Mother to mother, I know her fear.

"No," I promised. "No one's going to take her away."

Then I sat and listened to Joelle's description of her fury. I wondered if this was her first time saying it out loud.

"I did things I never imagined I would do. When [my daughter] was little, the fourth or fifth time she'd woken up in the night, I'd get in her face, saying, 'WILL YOU GO TO SLEEP?' God, it's awful, isn't it?" Joelle cut herself some slack for a brief moment, admitting the bulk of parenting falls on her, then immediately chided herself, "But I'm nowhere near as patient as my partner." Later in the interview, I learned her partner parents their daughter for one hour in the evenings, after he gets home from work at six (except for "football Thursdays"). Then Joelle puts their daughter to bed because the daughter prefers that she do it.

If the person going through matrescence is married to a good man or even a mediocre one, there is the added gaslighting experience that her anger from overwhelm and overwork will not be seen as legitimate because her husband is "one of the good ones." Twenty-first century men are supposedly more "woke" to feminism and are more involved in family life than their own fathers were. It's true that American dads today spend an average of seventeen hours a week on childcare and housework, which is almost triple that of fathers in the 1960s (six and a half hours). But when we compare modern dads to modern moms, who put in thirty-one hours a week on childcare and housework (not including the mental load and emotional labor), we are still a long way off from domestic equality.

If a father makes dinner a few times a week, mothers can feel like their primary parent struggles aren't real or don't matter. It is harder for a mother to voice her frustrations and feelings of overwhelm about all she is loaded down with because, well, it's mostly invisible, and because she has that golden unicorn—a man who cooks! But women still spend twice as much time preparing meals as men. Men might fry up the eggs, but their wives noticed they were running low, put them on the grocery list, did the meal planning for the week (including which dishes her husband would make on his nights), did the grocery shopping, unloaded the groceries, threatened the kids to get off their screens and set the table *right now*, harassed them to help clear the table, loaded the dishwasher, rescrubbed the pan after her husband rinsed it, and remembered to put soap in the dishwasher and actually turn it on before passing out for the night. The bar for fathers is still so low. Because Lauren's husband is the kind of guy "who makes an effort to ask how people are," when Lauren complains to others that he does not parent responsibly, she says, "People literally disbelieve me."

This kind of cultural gaslighting is not new. Women expressing dissatisfaction with the patriarchal status quo have long been discounted and associated with madness. In "Women and Hysteria in the History of Mental Health," the authors explain that in Greek mythology, when the virgins of Argo refused to "honor the phallus," Melampus "cured" the virgins' madness with hellebore, "then urged them to join carnally with young and strong men." Lack of orgasms and "uterine melancholy" were listed as the causes for this madness, named *hysteria* from the Greek word *hystera*, which means uterus. In his dialogue *Timaeus*, Plato argues that "the uterus is sad and unfortunate when it does not join with the male and does not give rise to a new birth," effectively making *more* phallus and patriarchy the cure for women's unhappiness with the phallus and patriarchy.

The *Ebers Papyrus*, a preserved medical document from Ancient Egypt dating from around 1550 BCE, describes one of the symptoms of hysteria as "the sense of suffocation." Hysteria stopped being considered a legitimate women's psychological condition by the 1980s, but the term suffocation is right on in the context of Motherhood. There's the monotony-induced suffocation of caring for young children and the way a mother's life becomes watching the hour hand on the clock move imperceptibly slowly, only to be interrupted by the prepping, serving, and cleaning of a thousand meals that aren't for her. And then there is the suffocation of fitting her gloriously messy and multifaceted self into the constricting identity of Mother, which always has a silent "good" in front of it, because mothers are supposed to be all cooing and care, granola bars and Band-Aids in her purse.

Being a "good mom" and holding onto a sense of self (beyond the new mother-self) are antithetical. As motherhood sociologist Sophie Brock told me in an interview, "The current cultural conception of the (perfect) mother is defined through selflessness, so self-erasure is part of acquiring the new identity of 'mother.'" Losing our identities, then being told by the culture that we should be happy with this erasure, is not just a potential outcome of going through matrescence today; it's a *requirement*. Whereas other identities, like lawyer, knitter, and father, are seen as merely additions to the self, Mother creates an entirely new self.

A good mother is just an evolution of a good girl. If you want to be a good girl, do what you're told. Please your parents. Don't get dirty. *Sit still!* Be grateful, say thank you. Be humble, say please. *Close your mouth!* Please your teacher. Put your hand down. Mind your business. *Sshhhh!* Take notes. Know what others want. Be ready. Be friendly. *Smile!* Cross your legs. Date. Men, of course. Get one to propose. Say I do. Please your husband. Don't nag. *Keep it fun!* Have his babies. Get on the floor and play with them. *Don't complain!* Cook. Clean. Fold. Invite. Host. *Charm!* Please everyone. Coordinate. Manage. Endure. *Enjoy!*

"This is the female's first lesson in the school of patriarchal thinking and values," writes feminist theorist bell hooks. "She must be good to be loved. And good is always defined by someone else." "Good mother" is defined by Motherhood's PR team, the top triangle of the culture's hierarchy. It is racially and economically coded to disseminate and uphold white middle-class values: quiet, deferential to men and authority figures, conflict-avoidant, schedule-oriented, busy and producing, competitive (but only with women), and physically attractive according to white beauty standards (thin, blonde, young).

Because the definition of the PR team's good mother was crafted with white patriarchal middle- and upper-class values, the rejection of it can be a revolutionary act of self-preservation, particularly for mothers of color, immigrant mothers, queer mothers, and working-class and poor mothers. But the PR team's expectations for a good mother are so exhausting and oppressive that even straight white middle-class mothers have begun to outwardly reject them by claiming the title of "bad mom."

A mother might post on social media:

Fed the kids pizza for dinner for the 3rd night this week. #Badmom

Sure, this mother may have some real guilt about defaulting to pizza so often, but I'd bet she knows that feeding her kids pizza three times a week isn't what truly knocks the "good" off one's "good mother" title. This mom may recognize that "good mother" standards are unattainable, but intellectual understanding doesn't necessarily create inner change, especially when the external pressures and expectations are still there. School permission slips still need to be signed, the kids still need to be brought to doctor appointments, and dinner still needs to be produced or procured. By saying, "I'm a bad mom," mothers are putting out a wish—not that they'll one day be terrible mothers, but that they'll one day let themselves off the hook.

One problem with white middle-class women publicly claiming "bad mom" is that they ignore the race and class privilege that allows them to feel comfortable enough to publicly profess their so-called failings. Another is that the good mom/bad mom dichotomy (think stay-at-home moms vs. moms with paid jobs, breastfeeding moms vs. bottle-feeding moms, cry-it-out moms vs. co-sleeping moms) is just noise distracting from the white supremacist, patriarchal elephant in the room that devalues *all* mothers, while also placing an impossible load on their shoulders. "If nothing more," says Athan, "we have a responsibility to end the forced choice of a love-it or hate-it narrative that splits mothers rather than aids them in making meaning of their motherhood."

In the rat race to be a good mother, in between washing the lunch containers, doing the kids' hair, and folding folding folding the laundry, we sometimes see our other (non-mothering) selves flickering in the distance. "Take care of me!" they say. *Right, right, me!* we think, then sigh. Another person to take care of. We may even go so far as opening up our calendars to search for something we can shift or reschedule so that we might make plans with a friend, go to the gym, or see a doctor for the hip that's been troublesome since we became mothers. But the effort stalls before the target is reached. We've already spent all our "taking care" energy for the day. Depleted, we turn away from ourselves and slump into a cozy chair with some Netflix.

I was thirty-one when Ollie was born. Six months later, my three-year fellowship as a teaching artist at a high school for pregnant teens and at the local public library ended. Between trying to be a writer while full-time parenting a baby, then navigating Ollie's challenging behaviors once they started exhibiting at around eighteen months, I felt completely spent every day. I had no patience, no grace to offer, and no desire for anything other than alone time.

For the first time in our relationship, Paul and I were fighting a lot. Co-parenting turned out to be much harder than I anticipated. This surprised me. We are alike in many ways, both in check-box ways (race, class, religion, education) and in those special, harder-to-pinpoint ways (down for adventures, twinkly-eyed, close with our families of origin, thinking I'm hilarious). Neither of us adheres to a parenting style with a name. You could say we're alike in that we're both allergic to dogma and get rebellious when we sense someone is telling us what to do. We do what suits us. The problem is what suits one of us doesn't always suit the other.

Here's how that played out back then. I'd sing out, "Time for baaaath!" the second we were done eating dinner, and Paul would say, "Let's just give Ollie a little play time." Our parenting-style avatars would leap out of our bodies and clash swords. I'd see the succession of tasks that needed doing and I'd calculate how long each one takes, methodically working toward the end goal of Ollie's punim hitting the pillow at seven thirty, which was when I'd get a break from my Mother work. Paul, who works all day conducting therapy sessions with his psychiatry patients, just wants things to be "chill." His goal is the path of least resistance.

I'd be all, "We're the parents and we run the ship!"

And he'd be all, "We *are* running the ship, but you need to ease up a little."

And I'd be like, "Fine! Then *you're* in charge of getting Ollie to bed." Then I'd add, "At seven thirty."

"Fine," he'd say, generously not responding to my condescension with "I know what goddamn time our child goes to bed."

I'd go and rage-scrub the dishes, then lie on my bed and stare into my phone screen until he'd call me to kiss Ollie goodnight at 7:45. I'd kiss my dumpling boy all over, then sing him a lullaby. Sometimes I'd be so "chill" that when Paul and I would walk out of Ollie's room, I wouldn't even make a snide remark about the time.

Despite the constant labor I was engaged in at home—if I wasn't taking care of Ollie, I was arguing with Paul about how to best take care of Ollie—I felt purposeless. I hadn't pursued more teaching gigs because I wanted to put all my non-parenting time and energy (haha) into writing. But (surprise, surprise) I had no time or bandwidth for writing, so I hesitated to even call myself a writer. My entire self was being funneled into Mother. And for what? I didn't seem to be very good at it.

A few months after Ollie turned two, I finally threw a rope down to my pre-motherhood self so I could climb down and salvage the bones. I pushed aside my mom guilt, and Paul and I put Ollie in daycare four days a week so I could work. I forced myself to leave the house and write at coffee shops so I wouldn't let all the domestic motherhood "shoulds" steal away my writing time. I felt lost, intimidated by the blinking cursor and the blank white page. My writing muscle was weak. The only writing I'd done in the last two years were lists—grocery lists, to-do lists, Ollie birthday party invite lists. So I started writing lists about my life—which is to say, motherhood—because in the throes of matrescence, everything *is* motherhood, or at least motherhood-adjacent.

Eventually my café tinkering turned into a three-year literary public art project called #MomLists. I would handwrite these lists (some were more like numbered mini-memoirs) that held all my questions, frustrations, observations, and joys about motherhood.

Then I sewed on decorative paper as an overlay, attached a ribbon, and hung each list-turned-art-piece in a public place around the Bay Area: coffee shops, laundromats, yoga studios, playgrounds. I wanted to shove the reality of motherhood in people's faces. With each list, I was reclaiming my voice.

I wanted more of this loud and proud self. I'd missed me! As the writing flowed, I entered a second phase of coming out as queer. I had originally come out as bisexual to my family and friends eight years earlier, when Paul and I got engaged. I was afraid that as a cis woman marrying a cis man who identified as straight, I would be closeted forever if I didn't come out.

Unfortunately, I went right back into the closet after saying "I do." I didn't mean to. I wasn't ashamed, and I still desired women, but I wasn't sure quite how to be queer within the institution of monogamous marriage to a straight man. I had no examples of what this looked like. Paul and I are always assumed straight. This provides us with straight-passing privilege—protection from LGBTQ-related discrimination and violence. It also means an important part of me goes unseen. This invisibility (a phenomenon called bisexual erasure) is painful at times. It becomes a dogged act of will to feel known.

When Paul and I were out in the world together, it sometimes felt like I was acting a part in a play of my own making, performing straightness. The performance became more intense with the role of wife, and it felt like I was getting nailed into straightness with the role of Mother. Most of our friends were straight couples who all had babies around the same time. Paul and I found ourselves surrounded by a community of straight families. As Ollie turned from baby to toddler, and at age three into a full-on child, I felt the pull to be true to myself, partially so that I could be true to Ollie about who I am.

To not be assumed straight, I had two options. Option A was to come out constantly (to friends, neighbors, teachers, my kids' friends' parents). Or there was option B: visually signal I'm queer. Option B proved somewhat challenging as a femme person. While I love the shaved undercut look, my hair is just too thin for that to work. (I gotta hold onto every postpartum strand I've got left!) So I mostly went with option A, with a little bit of B thrown in where I could.

I held onto writing and queerness for dear life, as I slowly re-integrated my old self and my mother-self into one complete self over the next couple of years, one baby step at a time. I got a queer therapist, and I came out to all the new friends I'd made since my first coming out. I continued to hang up my arty motherhood lists. I came out on social media. I started submitting the lists and getting them published in literary magazines. I pinned a little rainbow flag onto my jean jacket. The local San Francisco weekly paper did a write-up about my list project. Paul realized he was queer, too, which made me feel less lonely in my skin, and gave us an exciting new connection point that we used to grow our queer community. I went on my first writing retreat since having a baby—joined by Paul and three-year-old Ollie—and every day when I left our little residency house to go to the writing studio, *I* got to be the one who waved goodbye to my beautiful family and walked out the door to go do my very important work.

Coming out and writing were poles for me to grab onto as the world spun beneath my feet. They gave me purpose beyond wiping butts and making meals. I was reorienting into a new self. A mother-self, yes. But more. For mothers in the throes of matrescence, I recommend the transformative power of creative practice. I also recommend queerness, but that's neither here nor there. A mom doesn't need to be a writer or queer to make space for herself, so she can gather all of her parts into her biggest, fullest, baddest (goodest!) self.

In the years that have passed, I've gotten lost in motherhood a few more times. But the self that I (re)built during those crucial years has sustained me through new phases of matrescence, so that I don't feel quite as disoriented or desperate. Identity building is essential but challenging work for mothers. Everything in society is against us exploring and nourishing our non-mother parts. Intensive mothering leaves us very little time to do anything for ourselves. The cultural narrative says mothers should be satisfied with lives solely devoted to caregiving. And if we're not, society gaslights us by telling us our dissatisfaction with our singular lives is a personal failure.

The PR team's indoctrination has sunk deep inside me. Though Paul says nothing when I leave for a weeklong writing residency, or hire a babysitter when Paul's out of town so I can go to the San Francisco Dyke March during Pride, I still feel guilty when I prioritize myself. But I try my best to push past that guilt. Because the alternative is the "great motherhood reduction"—my busy, complex, creative, sexual, intellectual self diminishing to a self-hating, snack-making nap warden. I refuse to march willingly into the Lost Mother Valley, silent but for the echoes of others' praise.

So far, we've covered the way the PR team's cultural narrative entraps mothers, and how that narrative is enforced by cultural gaslighting, which coerces mothers to publicly perform wellness as their former complex selves wither away. Because moms seem to "have it under control," and because our labor continues to benefit society, lawmakers and taxpayers have no real incentive—financial or otherwise—to invest in mothercare by improving the barely existent systemic infrastructure. And to top it all off, the bone-deep exhaustion from the ever-expanding caregiving requirements of intensive mothering obliterates mothers' energy to speak out or organize to change any of it.

These are the boxes piled high in the mom rage basement. Now I'll bring us back up to the kitchen to look with fresh eyes at what's going on individually when mothers rage.

5　THE MOM RAGE CYCLE

> The phenomenon of female anger has often been turned against itself, the figure of the angry woman reframed as threat—not the one who has been harmed, but the one bent on harming.
>
> —Leslie Jamison, "I Used to Insist I Didn't Get Angry. Not Anymore."

No. No! This is NOT happening again! I thought as I read and reread the typed letter the teacher at five-year-old Ollie's second preschool handed me at pickup one afternoon.

"The school is no longer a good fit."

Ollie had been diagnosed with sensory processing disorder just six months prior. Finally getting a diagnosis and gaining more understanding of why Ollie acted in certain ways did not make me less frustrated when he exhibited these behaviors. Like the day when I saw Ollie touching baby Mae's little leg so sweetly—and then, suddenly, not so sweetly, his white-knuckled hand squeezing her leg as hard as he could, her skin puffed up red on either side of it.

In moments like these, I rarely spoke gently, rarely said, "Oh no no, this is not how we touch people. Can you show me how we should touch a baby? Yes, that's exactly right. You're such a good big brother." Instead, I exploded. "What are you doing? Why do you want to hurt her?! Do you hear her crying?! Do you!?" He was so rough with her it scared me. Then I was emotionally rough with him. Had I become part of the violence? Did I cause it? The learning curve was so steep, and at the bottom were the three of us, tear-streaked and disconnected. All I wanted to do was lie down on my bed and cry, but with Paul at work, I was alone with two children who could not be unsupervised.

Sending Mae to her nanny share and dropping Ollie off at his preschool in the mornings created an essential break for my nervous system. Getting a break from me and having other caring adults to guide him was probably good for Ollie's nervous system too. I knew I was having trouble bringing the calm, patient nurturing that Ollie deserved. I relied on—*needed*—his teachers to love him, delight in his clever mind, laugh at his goofy humor, and take pleasure in his doughy hugs. Having other adults bask in the wonder of my kids—especially when parenting is challenging—has always been a gift beyond explanation.

"We've received complaints from other parents." When I read the letter from Ollie's co-op preschool, the adrenaline of my outrage overtook the immobilization of my dejection. I went into high gear. Paul and I requested a sit-down with the teachers. We came to the meeting armed to the teeth with indignation and entitlement. I'd looked through the preschool's bylaws and discovered they hadn't followed proper protocol in expelling a student. *Aha!* We were ready with our carefully bullet-pointed arguments and our bribery package:

- A full-time aide, who would stay by Ollie's side and give the teachers some relief. (We would cover the aide's pay, which would double the cost of preschool.)
- A behaviorist to train the teachers to best support Ollie's particular needs. (We would pay for this too.)
- A promise that we would immediately begin the process of getting Ollie assessed by the local public school district, which could get him a spot at a public preschool run by trained special education teachers. (This is something that could have happened as early as age three, before he was kicked out of his first preschool, if any of his teachers had informed us we had a right to this service.)

In addition to the teachers and Paul and me, the entire preschool co-op board was in attendance. As board secretary, I'd asked them to come as witnesses.

In the meeting, Paul was unemotional and lawyer-like, a perfect contrast to my spitting anger and intermittent sobbing. I could barely look at the teachers. *How dare you give up on Ollie!* I yelled in my head when they had the audacity to raise their eyes to meet mine. With the pressure of the board members' presence, our argument about their violation of the bylaws, combined with our bribery package, Paul and I left the meeting victorious. Ollie could stay.

"You were amazing!" Paul grinned, holding my hand.

"So were you! We were fucking badasses!" I declared proudly. We *were* badasses. And we were also full of middle-class, English-speaking, white-people privilege, with time and money to throw at the problem.

After months of assessments, the public school district offered Ollie a spot at a preschool with a special education teacher, but by this time, it was already April. With preschool graduation in two months, we chose to let Ollie finish the school year where he was. Lexi, the one-on-one aide we hired, coached Ollie to use his words instead of his body to identify, express, and regulate his emotions, and to be a compassionate leader. Lexi was so skilled she made herself obsolete, and for the last few weeks of the school year, Ollie thrived all on his own.

After a few months' reprieve from the hard conversations with Ollie's teachers at pickup, I was breathing easier and feeling hopeful. Rage slipped from its number one slot in my list of problems.

Once a week, I saw Nat (my queer therapist, who I'd been seeing since my second coming out a few years before), but our sessions weren't dedicated exclusively to my rage. I had a whole life that needed tending! My relationship with Paul was strained by my rage, but also by the sheer exhaustion and stress of parenting two young kids. I was overwhelmed with navigating Ollie's school and health services. I still struggled with being queer in a hetero-appearing marriage. Not to mention how badly I wanted my writing career to flourish despite my minimal time and energy. With all these issues and more, it was easy to steer my therapy sessions with Nat toward anything that didn't focus on my monstrous rage or bottomless caverns of shame.

In my deft avoidance of confronting my rage that summer, it swelled. I'd signed Ollie up for two weeks at Dragon Adventures, a day camp he'd never been to before. It turned out that the staff, many of whom were teenagers, were not trained to work with neurodivergent children. Though Lexi had gotten Ollie to a place in his preschool where he could function happily and appropriately without her, here, in this new setting, problems arose on day one. *He's being too rough. He's putting his body on the CIT's body and the CIT* (counselor-in-training) *is uncomfortable.* Of course, I argued (or "advocated," as Nat would gently reframe): "You have to train your CIT to use words. Teach him to say to Ollie, 'I don't like how you're touching me. My body needs space.'" But my suggestions for their barely pubescent staff member were not a real training. By the end of the first week, my cell phone buzzed with the final call.

"Please come pick up Ollie." He and another kid had gotten physical, hitting and throwing each other onto the ground. The counselors told us not to return. I couldn't believe we were here again. School after school, camp after camp. It felt like everyone was saying my boy isn't good, isn't right, doesn't fit. *My boy IS good!* I wanted to scream. *He's GOOD! Please love him! Please don't give up on him! See his gentle, sensitive heart, his wild curiosity, and his big love. Please SEE him! See his good self.*

Inside those inner pleas was all my fear. *Is he okay? Will he be okay? Will he succeed in the world? Will people love him? Will he ever get a handle on appropriate physical behavior and stop touching people too roughly or without asking?* In retrospect, I also know that, because I was—and still am—so entangled with my children, with their feelings, their bodies, and their lives, inside that plea of wanting the world to see that Ollie is good was a plea for myself: *I am good. A good mother. I am struggling. Please see me. See my good self.*

It was just luck, or maybe it was the "divine universe" delivering exactly what I needed, that I began working with a life coach the same summer Ollie was kicked out of Dragon Adventures. My cousin Julia, who started a program that summer to become a life coach, told me the students in her program needed clients to practice working with. *I have Nat already. Do I really need a life coach too?* I thought skeptically. But when Julia told me Fran was queer, married to a rabbi, and moonlit as a drag queen, I couldn't resist.

I sobbed uncontrollably through my entire first session with Fran. I guess I needed a fresh face and permission to focus completely on my rage. My sobbing became a staple of our sessions.

Fran—round-faced, pink-cheeked, and not yet a parent—was gracious and empathetic as he passed me tissues and gently assigned me reading homework, which I scoffed at. But, ever the diligent student, I read the pages he gave me.

Though Fran and I only worked together for six months, our sessions set me on a years-long course of mom rage inquiry. By the time I met with Fran, I was beginning to understand that moms in our culture are rendered invisible and treated poorly by every societal structure. Fran brought me out of the basement and into my body with a pivotal piece of writing, a section of Daniel Goleman's book *Emotional Intelligence* called "Anatomy of Rage." This piece showed me there is rhyme and reason to my experience of rage. In addition to the cultural factors from my mom rage basement that are at play when I yell until I'm animal-growling, I'm also having a complex experience in my body and psyche. Goleman's work made me curious about how rage works as a physiological and psychological experience.

It has taken me nine years of trial and error on my own mom rage journey, countless hours of reading and research, and support from a wide range of professionals for me to understand that mom rage has structure beyond blind fury. I learned that the particular way most women are raised to experience and (not) express anger is a key component of mom rage. I came to understand that mom rage gestates and builds long before it emerges into a maelstrom of scream and bang. Mom rage is not just a boom followed by a weighted blanket of regret—it's a complex, multiphase cycle.

If we look at when Ollie squeezed baby Mae's leg, it appears to be a singular moment. But the Mom Rage Cycle includes the many times prior to my explosion that I smoothly intercepted Ollie and told him, "Gentle with Mae." After many interceptions, I eventually felt wisps of anger but pushed them down. And when I no longer could, I raged. The explosion was followed by a period of feeling wretched for raging. Finally, there was the fix-it moment, when I apologized to Ollie, and we reconnected.

Let's take a look at each individual phase of the cycle.

PHASE 1: THE RAMP-UP

This is the building phase. Repeated aggravations and feelings of overwhelm slowly rise inside the mother. The building of rage can happen slowly, sometimes over days, even weeks. In this phase, a mom is not screaming her head off or banging her palm on the wall. Instead, she often inhabits her "best" mother-self, all syrup-voice and kind words. During the Ramp-Up, the mother may be totally unaware that she is a live wire. This phase has three underpinnings: stress and lack of support, poor sleep quality, and the inherent annoyingness of kids.

Lack of support and stress are connected. Stress is the likely outcome when mothers don't have proper support—emotional support, financial support, childcare, healthcare—and need to hold down a full-time job, then have to come home to what amounts to a second full-time job. Repetitive daily stress can result in a slew of physiological and psychological problems, from memory and concentration impairment (another potential cause of "mom brain"), to anxiety, depression, and headaches. These problems are particularly acute for poor mothers, single mothers, and mothers of high-needs children, all of whom are more likely to suffer from chronic stress. Unsurprisingly, one study found that it was common for mothers experiencing chronic stress to be hostile with their families.

In 2018, Christine Ou and Wendy Hall, both nurses and academics, published a comprehensive review of twenty-four studies of postpartum depression and anger. They found that across the studies, mothers "reported feeling let down by others, which contributed to their feelings of irritation and resentment. Lack of support from partners and relatives was associated with mothers' anger."

With stress and lack of support both independently leading to anger, it's no wonder modern Motherhood feels like a structure fire—it's positioned at the intersection of two leaking gas lines.

The lack of structural and familial support for mothers leads to another contributor to mom rage: poor sleep quality. Not enough sleep might seem like a standard parenting problem, but it's got dirty gender laundry in the basement. Motherhood's PR team has the entire culture convinced that mothers are the natural caregivers of children. This results in interrupted sleep being "a burden borne disproportionately by women," according to Sarah Burgard, director of the Population Studies Center at the University of Michigan. Her 2011 study showed that even after children no longer need a feeding in the night, the gendered sleep imbalance persists regardless of work status, even when the mother is the primary breadwinner. Moms in dual-earning male-female couples are still almost three times as likely as dads to report that their sleep is interrupted to take care of the baby. The length of each waking is also skewed by gender. Moms are up for an average of forty-four minutes, dads for an average of thirty. Between moms having multiple children and the variety of reasons kids wake in the night, lack of quality sleep can be in play for mothers for a *decade*.

While most would agree that not getting enough sleep invariably causes next-day crankiness, this was empirically demonstrated in a study published in 2019. The authors showed that people functioning on a sleep deficit had an increased tendency toward anger, which directly inhibited their ability to cope with frustrating situations. Without a proper night's sleep, mothers don't have the wherewithal to pause before responding to stimuli.

Lack of sleep turns us into instinctual animals—sensitive, irritable, and quick to roar.

In 2022, Ou and her colleagues published another study that investigated the relationship between sleep and anger in postpartum mothers. The results showed that poor sleep quality and feeling like their babies are not sleeping well are noteworthy contributors to mothers' anger. Out of 278 Canadian mothers with healthy babies between six and twelve months old, 31 percent reported intense anger levels, a higher percentage than those who reported depression (26 percent).

To assess the mothers' anger, Ou used the standard anger measurement tool created by psychologist Charles Spielberger called the State Anger Scale, which consists of approximately fifteen agree/disagree statements that measure temporary anger, such as "I feel like throwing something right now." To be considered angrier than average on the State Anger Scale, the subject has to test into or above the seventy-fifth percentile. Ou raised the bar for her study and only considered the participants to be angry if they tested into the ninetieth percentile or higher. Though Ou did not use the word *rage* to describe the mothers in her study, she did say that her scale indicated they were "intensely angry." "So many women being so angry points to, yes, this is a problem," she concluded.

Both Paul and I wet the bed beyond the average age when we were children. I struggled with it well into fourth grade. Late bedwetting is a common symptom for kids on the autism spectrum. Between genetics and autism, Ollie never really had a chance. After Ollie sized out of Huggies' overnight pull-ups when he turned six, and we presented him with generic white ones with no cartoon drawing on the front, Ollie said no way.

Without a diaper, Ollie promptly began wetting the bed every night. We were constantly hauling sleepy, limp-bodied, sixty-pound Ollie to the toilet at night. We had tried taking him at ten thirty, before Paul and I went to sleep, but he still woke up wet in the mornings. So, for two years, Paul and I took turns setting an alarm and waking ourselves up in the middle of the night to take Ollie again. There was one brutal year where we were waking up both kids to pee at three in the morning.

In the end, my sleep was consistently interrupted for eight years. Whether we're waking up to nurse an infant, change a toddler out of wet pajamas, or comfort a kindergartener after a night terror, being a mother can severely throw sleep out of whack for years, leaving us bleary-eyed, exhausted, and teetering on the cusp of rage.

As though it's not enough to be stressed, undersupported, and exhausted, kids tend to know just how to push their parents' buttons over and over and over again. In *Emotional Intelligence*, Goleman cites the work of University of Alabama psychologist Dolf Zillmann, who discovered that rage can build over time from repeated aggravations, "a sequence of provocations." For example:

"Oh dear, please don't grab things off the shelves at the grocery store."

"Whoops, it's not safe to stand up in the cart."

"No more coming out of your room. It's nigh-nigh time."

"Don't call for me anymore. You close your eyes and have sweet dreams."

"This was my last time coming in here. Now Mommy needs to go to bed."

"I made lasagna for you."

"You *do* like lasagna. Remember you ate three pieces last week at dinner? You *love* lasagna."

"Yes, the whole thing has sauce on it, but not a lot. It's the same sauce that's on pizza."

"The green stuff is just basil. It's an herb, not a vegetable."

"No, Cheerios is not a dinner option tonight."

Motherhood is relentless provocation. When we consider how mothering requires us to soldier through months-long parenting phases of teeth-gritting frustration, we are truly saintly every time we manage to remain calm, gently steer, remind, redirect, teach, ask politely, and request firmly but without anger, over and over, and then do it again the next day and the next day and the next.

When we berate ourselves for losing our tempers later in the Mom Rage Cycle, what we are not doing is remembering the countless times during the Ramp-Up phase when we did not blow up. We tend to forget that *before* we gruffly grabbed their little wrists and bellowed, "STOP HITTING ME!" we gently held their pudgy hands and said in a nurturing, self-contained voice, "No, no, hands are not for hitting. Hands are for hugging friends." We erase all the times we kissed our little ones' fingers and tried to help them name their emotions. Though these stellar mothering moments slide right into the ether, they are part of the ramp-up to mom rage.

PHASE 2: EMOTIONAL WHACK-A-MOLE

In patriarchal societies, women are raised to be in service to men. The best way to serve the powers that be (the white supremacist, capitalist patriarchy) is to not disrupt or call attention to them. Don't ask why the board of directors has only one woman, one person of color, and no members who are gay. Don't point out that most employees who are mothers can't attend the company-sponsored happy hour. Marginalized groups and women learn throughout the course of our lives that if we don't cause a fuss or make a scene, if we are "nice," stay quiet, smile, keep our anger to ourselves, accommodate those around us, and generally let the status quo carry on—we will be rewarded for our likability. And if we don't keep our mouths shut when we feel we've been wronged, we will be punished for "causing problems."

Anger's cultural risks and rewards teach all people raised to be women to suppress our anger, but cultural identities like race and class are always at play. Writer Diamond Yao explains the double bind that diasporic Asian women face around anger: "For Asian women in the diaspora, the denial of our anger exists at the toxic intersection of sexism and the model minority stereotype, enforced on two fronts by white Western culture and from within our own communities." Under the institution of slavery, physical violence was used to maintain a power dynamic between owner and enslaved person that required the suppression of Black people's voices, including their anger. Family separation was another tactic used to try to destroy their personhood. This racist penalization of anger, voice, and personhood (all intimately connected) continued into the Jim Crow era and still exists today. The "angry Black woman" stereotype lowers the society's tolerance threshold for Black women's anger, and results in swifter, more severe punishment.

It can be difficult for people raised as girls to express rage when we've been taught from very early on that it is in our best interest to suppress our anger. It is culturally acceptable for women to be sad, not angry. In one study on gender, anger, and the workplace, the participants conferred higher status to sad female employees than to angry ones. For men the opposite was true. Men, particularly white men, are rewarded and forgiven for their anger, while women are penalized and blamed.

Ceci, the mestiza paralegal, now lives in Los Angeles with her husband, five-year-old son, and twenty-two-year-old stepdaughter. She described herself using the exact language of a woman who was taught by the culture not to value or express her anger: "I'm a people pleaser. I don't rock the boat. I go along with everything, do what people tell me." This is the path of being a good girl, a good woman, and eventually a good mother.

Lifelong gendered learning teaches people raised to be women to push down anger and any feelings in the "sub-anger" ballpark, such as annoyance, irritation, and frustration. I imagine this emotional push-down like the carnival game whack-a-mole. Each time an uncomfortable or unpleasant anger-related feeling pops up—*whack!*—women automatically bang it with a big-headed mallet, sending it back beneath the surface.

Like the rage itself, this game of anger whack-a-mole is an international phenomenon for women. In Korea, there is a culture-related anger syndrome called *hwa-byung*. It translates literally to "illness of fire" and mostly affects working-class middle-aged housewives, who have chronically suppressed anger stemming from strict gender roles, gender-based inequality, and patriarchal family structures. In traditional Latin American folk medicine, it is believed that holding onto certain emotions can cause physical illness. In Northeast Brazil, the term *engolir sapos* translates to "swallowing frogs," and is mostly used by women to refer to the suppression of anger and irritation, and the pressure to tolerate unfair treatment without complaint.

Cheryl, the Black civil rights lawyer who internalizes her mom rage, is practiced at playing whack-a-mole with her anger: "I'm good at repressing things. So, a little problem, I repress it, and it gets packed on top of all the other things that make me mad, until there's no way to untangle it. It's just this huge tangle of anger that I'm trying to disassociate from all the time."

In our present-day culture of busy, intensive motherhood, stuffing down unpleasant emotions can be a matter of practicality. Minutes are a precious resource, and airing every frustration is a time expense that modern mothers cannot afford. Emails must be sent, dinner needs to get into bellies, and bodies need to snuggle under covers. But the perceived time-saver of the Emotional Whack-a-Mole phase is a mirage. Every time a mom suppresses her angry feelings, as she's been taught to do her entire life, she is pushing them onto an ever-growing pile of anger inside her. Eventually, the pile will topple.

PHASE 3: RAGE

During this phase, all the aggravation buildup from the first phase and the whacked-down emotions from the second phase come bursting out in explosive, uncontrolled anger.

By the time a mom gets to phase three and loses control, she has been hard at work *not* raging, possibly for days. Dolf Zillmann's "series of provocations" means that each frustrating moment builds on the one before it, activating our adrenal gland, which releases the stress hormone cortisol into our bloodstream. Excess cortisol weakens the influence of our prefrontal cortex, a part of the brain responsible for a variety of things including judgment, decision-making, and self-control.

An experience Ceci had when her son was two and a half shows how a series of provocations can lead to rage. One night, before bed, Ceci's son had a screaming tantrum because he didn't want to take a bath (provocation number one). The next evening after a long day at work, Ceci picked her son up from daycare. He struggled against being strapped into his car seat, yelling and hitting her (provocation two). Once he was buckled and she was driving them home, Ceci's son began throwing whatever he could get his hands on at his mother (provocation three). After making it home safely, Ceci walked past her husband watching TV in the living room, and into the kitchen to discover her twenty-two-year-old stepdaughter's breakfast dishes still in the sink (provocation four). And then, Ceci had the realization that the next thing on her to-do list was making dinner for her whole family (provocation five). "In front of all of them, I started yelling and throwing things, like, 'What the fuck? Why do I have to do everything? Why? I'm tired! I'm fucking over it!' I just lost it."

Even after we explode, then cry, then apologize and complete the Mom Rage Cycle, Zillmann tells us that our nervous system does not return immediately—or even within the next twenty-four hours—down to a cool and collected starting point of zero. Instead, we move forward with elevated neurological arousal, possibly for up to a week, making another rage in the near future more likely.

Carrie is another mom I interviewed, and both she and her wife, Ameena, struggle with mom rage. Carrie is white and a social worker. Ameena is Egyptian and works in marketing. They identify as middle class and live in Sacramento, California, with their two sons, a trans boy, age seven, and a cis boy, age four.

Carrie says that when she's heading toward rage, her words get meaner and the volume of her voice gets louder. "It goes from anger-yelling to having violent thoughts that I would never act on. I'm just like, 'Oh my god, I want to close the door and not tell you' or 'I just want to throw you off of me.'"

The boys sometimes hit their moms, which often is the final straw that sends Carrie and Ameena into rages. "Our kids are very physical. They have tantrums with hitting and biting us." Carrie described a moment when her older son was coming out of the bathroom. "He kind of came at me. He either jumped on me or threw water at me, and I just pulled him off of me in a way that his t-shirt was around his neck, and it pulled. My rage is very animalistic. It's primal."

PHASE 4: THE SHAME SPIRAL

Carrie remembers that after she pulled her son off her, he said, "Ow, that hurt me," and touched his neck. "I felt such shame that I could have hurt him, and especially around his neck. I think the shame is, when they catch me off guard and I feel attacked, that I will defend myself as a priority over protecting them." Carrie's guilt floods her with fear: "Did I do something they're going to remember as hurtful? Could I have actually hurt them?"

The Shame Spiral occurs once the mother has come down from her fury, the "beast in her throat" gone. With the kids asleep and the constant din of a household with small children now quieted, the mom scrolls through pictures on her phone, staring at her kids' faces. She yearns for the smell of their freshly cleaned hair, the feel of their chubby hands wrapped around her in a hug. They are her biggest loves and most special creatures she is privileged to care for. Tears flow as shame and guilt take hold.

With the shame, negative self-talk arrives. *How could I have yelled like that?* The mother recalls her child's face when she yelled. *I scared her,* she thinks ruefully. *What kind of role model am I? I should be able to be calm. I am the worst mother.* Maybe the mom tries to reach out to friends, writing and deleting text messages about how awful she feels. In lieu of connection, she watches TV and eats chocolate, vowing to control herself better next time.

Self-isolation is a key component of the Shame Spiral for me. I am so deep in my own sorrow and self-hatred after a rage, I have a hard time reaching out to friends. I know I am in a healthier place—less far down the spiral—when I allow myself to be worthy of love and forgiveness by pressing *send* on the text messages to my mom friends.

Paul, on the other hand, I won't let near me—which is easy because he doesn't seem to want to come close anyway. Often my rages at the kids are when he isn't around, because his presence—really anyone else's presence—mitigates my outbursts. Because I am embarrassed by my rage, I am better able to keep my rage in check when other people are nearby. If Paul is around for the Shame Spiral, it feels like we are repelling magnets, staying on opposite ends of our small house. If we're both in our bedroom, we'll lie on the bed turned away from each other, earbuds pushed tight into our ears, escaping into our own private screens. Neither of us has any empathy for me. I have just raged at our most precious babies, or possibly at Paul. I both desperately want him to rub a warm hand on my arm and know that I would not be able to accept such kindness, because in this dark shame place, I am certain I do not deserve it.

Brené Brown, author and shame researcher, says, "The enemy of worthiness is shame." She defines shame as "the intensely painful feeling or experience of believing that we are flawed and therefore unworthy of love and belonging." With all the work Motherhood's PR team has put into cultural messaging, every one of us has internalized that aside from abandoning or abusing one's children, angry is the worst thing a mother can be. Modern motherhood leads us directly to the precipice of fury, and when we inevitably rage, everything we've ever been taught about how mothers are supposed to be makes us curl into a ball of self-hatred and shame.

Carrie and Ameena experience the Shame Spiral phase as a whistleblower of sorts. When they feel shame, it confirms for them that they were acting out of control—raging. Because Carrie and Ameena both have mom rage, they can more easily access empathy and understanding when the other rages. As a result, their experience of the Shame Spiral does not include the isolation I feel in mine. Carrie said the one who raged is able to be vulnerable and say to the other, "I feel so bad about how I handled that."

"My goal is for my children to feel held and supported and contained," Carrie said. She knows this is Ameena's goal, too, so when she's feeling ashamed, she goes to Ameena and asks how she can be better.

Carrie and Ameena's story inspires me. It demonstrates that if we can manage to not get bogged down by it, the Shame Spiral has the potential to help mothers be more self-aware and use their vulnerability as a springboard to reach for support. The fourth phase can last anywhere from a few minutes to a few days, depending on the severity of the rage episode and the length of time until the mother repairs with the person or people she raged at.

With amends and time, the bulk of the shame dissipates. But a small piece, a tiny sharp-edged stone can remain. A seventy-four-year-old mother, whose "hyperactive boys" are now in their forties, sent me a message revealing the shame stone she still carries. "Even though my boys grew up and are great, I still feel guilt for that mom rage I felt. I've been having nightmares."

PHASE 5: SHORT-TERM REPAIR

Because mom rage is a product of big cultural structures, fixing it will require fixing those structures. I'll offer some suggestions about how we might begin to think about that work later in this book. In the meantime, there's short-term repair: the work mothers do to reconnect and repair their relationships post-rage.

Short-Term Repair takes place when the mother's emotional state has stabilized. She is no longer seething and has risen at least partway out of the depths of her shameful despair. In this phase, the mother reestablishes connection with the recipient of her rage, until both parties feel secure again in their attachment.

"I'm sorry I yelled at you. Even when I'm upset, you do not deserve to be yelled at," and other similar apologies act as reassurance that the mom's rage is not the rage recipient's fault. Her apology must take full responsibility for her behavior. It cannot blame the rage recipient by having a "but" attached, as in, "I'm sorry I got so mad, *but* you need to clean up after yourself."

Provided the rage recipient gives consent, a gentle touch such as a hug, holding hands, or rubbing can also be healing. Studies have shown the positive results of touch on people's performance ability, survival, and happiness levels. Gentle touch can release oxytocin, help create trust, and lower our cortisol levels. Touch can also relax the prefrontal areas in our brains, which regulate emotions. Science journalist Benedict Carey said it this way: "In effect, the body interprets a supportive touch as 'I'll share the load.'" When a mother is ready to repair, she is able to help release the emotional load her rage recipient might be carrying.

Listening to rage recipients helps them know their feelings and experiences are valued and important to the mother. If the person the mother raged at is her child, she might ask, "How did you feel when I slammed the door earlier? What did you feel in your body?" Listening can be painful. It's when Mae might say, "You scared me, Mama," or tell me that it made her tummy hurt or her heart beat fast. I have to work to stay in Mae's experience, and not get pulled out by my shame clouds gathering again overhead. It's okay if I cry, but I need to keep it to a few tears and not break down in heaving sobs. What matters is listening and making Mae feel seen and held by an emotionally regulated adult.

Maggie, a Taiwanese American mom of twin five-year-old girls living in Southern California, uses a child-appropriate repair practice she calls "listening circles." Anyone in the family can call for a listening circle. Whoever calls it speaks first, and the others have to look at the speaker and listen without talking until it is their turn. This is not without challenge. Sometimes Maggie wants to jump in and say, "Well, I did that because you did this thing!"

To encourage her twins to express themselves if they feel upset by something their parents said or did, Maggie tells them, "I might not be happy in the moment, but I'll be okay with it. And you might be mad at me, but I'm still gonna love you."

There have been times when Maggie has raged, or when she and her husband are in an argument, and her kids have called a listening circle. If Maggie is irate or in a place where she knows she will not be able to hear them, she tells them she's not ready yet, and her family waits until she is. One of her kids might say in the listening circle, "Mommy, I didn't like how you talked to me. You were not kind, and you're scaring me." Maggie admits it can be pretty uncomfortable. "But at the same time, I'm like, 'You know what? I'm glad you said something. I'm sorry. I'm tired and cranky.'" Maggie said the listening circles have sensitized her to the power of her words and tone.

While they aren't easy, Maggie admitted the listening circles have become a practice ground for the entire family to recognize their feelings and express them out loud. "I think the shame I feel after I rage comes from a place of thinking I am bad for being angry, bad for yelling. The listening circles have taught me that if I show my children a range of feelings, they'll show me a range of their feelings. And none of the feelings are bad."

This phase of the cycle offers an opportunity to exemplify making mistakes and learning from them in order to grow and do better next time. When I'm repairing with Ollie, this might sound like, "You know how you are trying hard to remember to ask before you touch people? Well, I'm working on something too. I'm working on getting better at staying calm even when I get scared or overwhelmed." Then I can share a strategy I'm going to start trying, like walking to the sink and splashing my face with cold water to reset my nervous system, or breathing in through one nostril and out the other to center myself when

I edge toward boiling. I am not very practiced at these sorts of calming techniques, but that's okay. I am reminding not just Ollie but myself that I don't have to be good at something or know it will be a sure bet to give it a try. Just talking about it is useful because it makes the moment shareable and interactive. We can practice deep breaths together. One of us might snort. We might giggle. This is how we return to each other.

I might ask Ollie, "What are some things you do to keep yourself calm when you get upset?" This kind of inquiry lets Ollie teach me and show off his knowledge and skills. It gives him confidence and opens up a pathway for future dialogue between us.

Repair is a key part of the cycle. If mothers skip this step and return to business as usual, acting like the rage never occurred, both parties miss out on the opportunity for healing, forgiveness, and reconnection. Without proper repair, the rage recipient—especially if they are a child—may think that the mother's rage is their fault, that they are bad or deserving of such treatment.

Psychologists John Gottman and Robert Levenson researched married couples in conflict and found that marriages were healthy and more likely to survive if there were five positive interactions between the couple for every negative interaction. They called this the Magic Relationship Ratio. Other psychologists have since expanded this five-to-one ratio as a guidepost for healthy parenting. Though my feelings of overwhelm, stress, and resentment are legitimate, I still don't want my children's experience of me to be one that is full of rage. The more positive interactions we have with our loved ones—kind words, engaged listening, gentle touch, apologizing, play—the more likely our rage will not cause long-lasting damage.

Barbara, a mixed-race Latina who does not have kids, grew up in a middle-class American household with a mother who raged. Now in her thirties, Barbara said, "My mom is the first person [my brother and I] want to celebrate with, go to when we need help or advice. And we trust and love her and my dad so fully." Barbara remembers her mother always came to them after a rage and hugged them tightly, said she was sorry, and cried. While the repair process was helpful, Barbara says that, as with the Magic Relationship Ratio, it was the consistent positive interactions Barbara and her brother had with their mom the majority of the time that ensured the longevity of their loving relationship. "She was always there for us, advocated for us, clearly wanted us to be happy, and expressed a lot of affection, praise, and pride in us. Even with the rage stuff, I never felt like my mom didn't love me a ton. [The rages] just felt like interruptions to be weathered."

When I sit with my children in our own little repair circle, I fill with the chatter of Ollie's and Mae's small voices, their even, open gazes, our fingers dancing on each other's legs. I can sense the okayness returning to our attachment. They are okay. I am okay. We are okay. I swell with such love for them. I can feel theirs too. It is in this moment that my walls come down and I am finally able to accept love, and complete the Mom Rage Cycle.

6 INVITE YOUR RAGE TO TEA

Rage—whether in reaction to social injustice, or to our leaders' insanity, or to those who threaten or harm us—is a powerful energy that, with diligent practice, can be transformed into fierce compassion.

—Bonnie Myotai Treace, "Rising to the Challenge: Filling the Well with Snow"

I was six months pregnant with Mae when my therapist Nat went on her own maternity leave. I loved being pregnant together, our eyes and growing bellies staring at each other as we engaged in careful listening and questioning for fifty minutes every week. I was happy for Nat to become a mother, and selfishly happy for myself. Though I always felt seen and heard by her, I thought, *Now she'll really understand when I talk about motherhood.* In our final session before her three-month leave, Nat handed me a slip of paper that said "Rachel" with a phone number underneath. Rachel had a psychotherapy practice just across the hall from Nat.

I took the paper but waved my hand flippantly. *I'm not* that *bad off*, I thought.

Ollie was three and a half and already using his body in problematic ways. Once, in anger, he head-butted me so hard I thought my nose was broken. Potty training was not going well. The brutality of pickups was in full swing at his first preschool. Ollie was still undiagnosed, and it hadn't occurred to Paul or me that we should get him evaluated. I just thought he was "spirited," and none of his teachers ever said to me, "Hey, maybe you should get this sweet boy checked out to see if anything in particular is going on."

The three months Nat was on leave were the same three months that culminated in Ollie's teacher at his first preschool telling me they'd never seen anything like this and didn't really know what else to do, which is a nice albeit indirect way of saying, "Please leave." One could argue it was also an indirect way of saying we should get him evaluated, but if that's what was intended, it didn't land. On top of all this, I'd gained seventy pounds during my pregnancy with Mae, so I was uncomfortable and exhausted. My parenting capacity hovered at zero.

During this time, I would rage at Ollie in the car on the way home from preschool after receiving the more difficult reports of his behavior. "Why did you do that!" I'd exclaim. I must have asked that question a thousand times, in every octave, up and down the decibel scale. Ollie didn't know why, so he wouldn't respond. His silence infuriated me. It scared me too. I would yell until he cried. Bang on the steering wheel. If I was driving, sometimes I'd pull the car over suddenly. I wanted to scare him, to get through to him, to make him cry. I needed to see that he felt something! Maybe remorse! If he felt bad, maybe he wouldn't body slam a small child or scratch through a teacher's skin again. Once his tears came, mine followed. *What have I done? He is just a three-year-old boy,* I would think, then I'd park and get out, un-buckle Ollie, and wrap my arms around him.

"I'm so sorry I yelled. Mommy shouldn't yell at you. I love you. I know you're sorry. I'm sorry." His chubby, tear-streaked face would nuzzle against me. We'd hold each other, then drive home, emotionally spent.

"Hi Rachel, I'm Nat's client. Do you have any availability this week?"

Like with Fran, whose sessions I would sob through two years later, I cried for the entire first therapy session with Rachel as I recounted my rage and what a terrible person I was. I returned a week later and cried for much of that appointment too. Toward the end of our third session, Rachel said she wanted to talk about the way I treat myself.

"I don't want to talk about that. I need to deal with the rage! I have to stop raging at my kid!" I said sharply.

Unruffled by my intensity, Rachel held my gaze and said, "I think the way you treat yourself is directly connected to your rage."

For complicated reasons, I didn't get to work with Rachel again, but her words outlasted our brief relationship. She hit on something I've rarely viewed as a problem—my perfectionism and my self-punishing nature when I don't meet the high bar I set for myself.

I am chronically early. Even after becoming a mother and schlepping around two young kids with their own agendas, I still show up when and where I say I'm going to. When they were young, I'd have a diaper bag packed with everything we could possibly need for an unexpected situation, like a diaper blowout or an apocalypse—extra outfits, an emergency bottle of formula in case we got stuck in traffic and baby Mae started screaming, enough snacks for a lifetime, an inflatable canoe, etc.

Prior to having children, I never viewed my perfectionism as a problem. Over-preparedness, anticipating what others might do, say, or want, arriving early, being well-dressed, doing all my reading homework without skipping even a footnote—these are the things that help people succeed, especially women. Perfectionism is a trait I've learned through the gender training of white supremacy culture. The various gatekeepers in life (often white, wealthy, straight, cis men) are even less likely to wave me through if I'm deemed by their standards as unprepared, unimpressive, or unattractive.

Motherhood reveals all the aspects of ourselves we need to work on. I now see the ways I place my perfection-seeking, high standards and subsequent critical nature on my children and all the people I love. My best friend, a mom of two little kids, admitted to me once that she is afraid to flake on me when we have plans because I will get upset. My internal reaction was, *Good! You shouldn't flake on me! It's disrespectful of my time. I also have two young kids.* Her confession was a plea for me to give her room to be imperfect. She was asking for leniency. Sometimes the rope I hold is so taut, it feels like I can't give any extra, not to my friends, not to my family, and especially not to myself.

In Ou and Hall's comprehensive review of research on postpartum depression and anger, they write, "Although several authors argue that postnatal women's anger was directed towards the self, self-critical mothers also directed anger outwards because they held others to standards they held for themselves."

Failure is the only outcome in the game of perfection. I don't want the people I love to feel pressed to live up to my standards of the perfect friend/partner/child, and then inevitably feel like failures. I want to offer a love that is spacious, not punishing. My perfectionism combined with my anxiety makes me want to control things. If I am the one in control, then things will go well, because I have done the necessary legwork to *make* them go well. Unfortunately, motherhood doesn't give a rat's ass about my plans or my fucking legwork. Nor do my children. It is the moment when they *do* care that I am afraid of. Will it mean I have finally taught them good executive functioning? Or will it mean I have succeeded at bringing them into my perfectionist anxiety and made them just like me? Is even asking this question an example of the way I punish myself? Or are these the self-aware questions of a mother trying not to ruin her children with her perfectionism—which contributes to her critical nature, which contributes to her rage?

Motherhood can be a dark place for a perfectionist. With its 180-degree learning curve, its isolation, its never-ending, primary-parent responsibilities combined with societal expectations that we are naturally supposed to be great at mothering despite zero training and subpar support, perfectionism shouldn't be capable of surviving in motherhood. Yet, like ants in the house during the first big rain of the year, even when we think the messy inevitability of motherhood has stamped out every last ounce of perfectionism, more comes crawling out from cracks we didn't even know existed.

When Rachel connected the dots between the way I treat myself and my rage, it showed me that I needed to pull my rage close and see what else might be swimming around in there. I raged regularly, yet I was so afraid of my rage, so embarrassed and ashamed of it, I didn't really know anything about it. How could I think about engaging with the long-term repair work of alleviating mom rage on a systemic and cultural level without doing the internal work to understand more about the blueprint of my own personal rage?

I decided to invite my rage to tea. Instead of disparaging my mom rage and pushing it as far away from consciousness as possible, I did something harder—I welcomed it in with curiosity and generosity, the way I would a guest at my table.

WOO WARNING

Though I love and respect ritual, I'm generally wary of all things woo. I don't think "putting things out into the universe" *actually* makes them more likely to happen. I don't do crystals. I didn't read *The Secret*. I don't go to full moon ceremonies, unless they're paired with an excellent DJ and the promise of potent psychedelics. I don't put any stock in fate, an afterlife, magic, God, or ghosts. But I also hold the door ajar for those things, because I don't feign to know what's out there beyond what I can see. I am not strict in my anti-woo, just skeptical. I believe people should do what serves them, so long as it doesn't cause harm.

In the following section, I personify and converse with my rage. I don't do this to be cute or witchy or woo. I do it because it helps me view my rage not as a hovering evil I want nothing to do with, but as a useful source of information. That reframing is the most useful thing I've figured out for how I experience mom rage.

———

My rage rapped loudly on the door. I ushered her in, took her coat and pulled out a chair. I set tea down in front of her, thick with milk and honey, and opened the good tea cookies Paul insists on buying. I was surprised how willing she was to talk to me, how eagerly she spoke about herself. She was animated, crumbs falling from her lips onto her lap as she gestured with her hands. Her dark eyes sparkled and her voice carried. *She's Jewish*, I thought, delighted. It felt like meeting a long-lost sister for the first time. *I know you*, I thought. And by the open way she spoke, I could tell she knew me too.

I discovered that if I could set down my shame and self-hatred, even just temporarily, and view my rage with respect and kindness, I could actually hear what she was trying to tell me. Ruth King, meditation teacher and author of *Healing Rage: Women Making Inner Peace Possible*, wrote to me, "Rage is not to be understood as a useless emotion, empty of story or knowledge. Rather, rage is fierce clarity and untapped fuel. Embraced with compassion, the energy trapped in rage becomes an intimate and empathic teacher."

King's reframing of rage falls in step with Audre Lorde's thinking about anger a quarter of a century earlier: "Anger is a source of empowerment we must not fear to tap for energy rather than guilt. When we turn from anger we turn from insight, saying we will accept only the designs already known, those deadly and safely familiar." Mothers keeping their anger in a locked trunk supports the white supremacist capitalist patriarchy—the PR team—the designs already known. For people who are systemically oppressed, including mothers, anger holds danger and power in its potential for individual and cultural change. Anger is a weathervane pointing to the places that need attention and healing.

In order to see my rage as a teacher, I needed to become her student by asking questions. I could not bring myself to speak aloud to my rage—the woo factor was just too high for me—so instead, we had a written conversation in my journal. In much the same way that I get more detailed information from my children about their school day when I ask open-ended questions, I get better answers from my rage when I steer clear of yes-or-no questions.

Here's what I asked my rage:

Where does it hurt? This question spears right to the vulnerability hiding beneath my wrath. When I rage, I can't access my hurt places. By the time the anger train has left the station, I am miles away from my initial wounds of feeling disrespected, alone, powerless, and not good enough.

What are you afraid of? Asking about fear similarly disarms my anger and flips it onto its back, exposing the velvety underbelly. When I rage at my kids for getting rowdy in their play or crossing a street without me, underneath my anger is usually fear that their bodies are going to get hurt. Sometimes my anger at a single moment is blown out of proportion because I'm afraid if I allow Ollie to do something one time it will mean he will always try to push that boundary. When five-year-old Ollie used to beg me to cross streets without holding my hand, I'd think, *If I let my kid cross this small street one time without holding my hand like he wants, he will never allow me to hold his hand again and crossing streets will become a power-struggle nightmare!*

What are you trying to protect? This can be related to the fear, but having different words can be useful in accessing the intimacies of rage. Sometimes, there's something I hold sacred that I am afraid is at risk. It is often my time: non-parenting time, alone time, exercise time, writing time, time with a friend.

What do you need? With Paul, it often boils down to needing to feel like I'm not alone, that we are on a parenting team together, or that I'm being considered when he makes decisions. With the kids, my needs vary. If I hear my kids screaming, which they tend to do when their sibling play is getting really fun (read: physical and out of control), my whole body tenses up. Their screams serve as a warning bell that someone, probably Mae, is moments away from getting hurt. I experience the fear and auditory overload as a desperate need—*the screaming has to stop now.*

My challenge was to write down my rage's responses without judgment. I found myself wanting to argue and point out that her answers were problematic. For example, when I ask the kids to come inside for dinner and they don't respond and remain outside, she told me she needs a verbal response from them in order to feel heard and not feel disrespected. I wanted to argue with her that the kids not saying, "Okay, Mom, just a second," wasn't a good enough reason to lash out. But I'm glad I didn't argue my way out of writing it down. Later, it would emerge as a useful clue. Writing my rage's answers provided me with a living document of the needs, fears, and hurt places that live inside my rage. After making a practice of this for a couple months, patterns emerged. I noticed that most of my rage stems from the same few things.

Next, I parsed through my rage further. If I could keep my self-criticism at bay, let my curiosity lead, and remain an empathic listener, I could become an expert observer of my own experience. After all, nobody knows my mom rage better than I do.

I zeroed in with more specific questions, in search of clues that would reveal structure, sequence, or order to my rage:

Location: Are there certain places I tend to rage? The bathroom? The car? On vacation? At the playground? In the kitchen?

Other people: Do I rage only in private? The day after I visit my in-laws? After the kids spend time with specific friends?

Times of day: What time of day am I raging? Before I've had my morning coffee? When the kids are hyper and tired just before dinner? During bath time and toothbrushing?

Other contributing factors: When is the last time I ate? How did I sleep the night before? Am I stressed about money? When's the last time I had a couple hours of alone time? When did I last have sex? When's the last time I exercised? Have I been getting enough writing time? Have I been social with my friends?

The more I tracked my experience, the more I understood my personal rage risk factors.

Finding patterns was almost—dare I say—fun! It pushed me into a different headspace about my rage. Instead of being paralyzed by shame, I was busy logging my observations. Inviting my rage to tea helped me separate from it. The distance made it possible for me to hold her like a crystal ball, turning my rage in my hands—an in-depth examination of this unique, volatile creature who requires care and attention.

Once I got smarter about my rage, I went from making observations to testing my hypotheses in hopes of generating change. Inviting my rage to tea showed me that toothbrushing holds explosive properties for me.

Here's how toothbrushing can look when three-year-old Mae, seven-year-old Ollie, and I are crammed into our broom-closet-sized bathroom. The two of them have spitting competitions and dance around, knocking elbows, till they have completely swapped brushing for wiggling, spitting, and laughing. Someone inevitably gets hurt. I usually begin with "Two feet on the floor when we brush. Stay on your side of the sink." But by the end of the two minutes, my hands roughly grab Mae's body to move her to her side of the sink while screaming, "Brush your teeth!"

Inviting my rage to tea helped me realize that I could try something new and possibly not embody the toothbrushing tyrant for a day or more. Now, when bath time is ending and I know toothbrushing is next, I ask myself, *Will toothbrushing destroy you today?* And if the answer is yes, instead of judging myself for being impatient and desperately needing my kids to go to bed so I can be horizontal for the rest of the night, I say to Mae, "I'm going to brush your teeth tonight!" She responds in her pretend baby voice, "Mama brush!" and happily climbs onto my lap. Ollie does a much better job without his partner in crime next to him. Brushing done, screaming averted.

When we listen to our rage, we pay homage to our anger. While raging at our loved ones is not ideal, we are entitled to all our emotions. "Anger has a bad rap," says Soraya Chemaly, author of *Rage Becomes Her: The Power of Women's Anger*. "But it is actually one of the most hopeful and forward thinking of all our emotions. It begets transformation, manifesting our passion and keeping us invested in the world. It is a rational and emotional response to trespass, violation, and moral disorder." Anger is an appropriate response to the expectations of high intensity mothering in a white supremacist, homophobic, classist, ableist, xenophobic, transphobic, misogynist, capitalist patriarchy that doesn't value care work or recognize mothering as essential labor, without which the society would fall apart.

So while toothbrushing itself is not trespass, violation, or moral disorder, it is the final straw at the end of a long day, a long week, a long month, a long year, a long motherhood that is steeped in trespass, violation, and moral disorder.

Part of inviting my rage to tea is about healing my perfectionism and the hateful ways I treat myself when I don't hit that "perfect mother" bar. If I pull back the curtains on my rage, poke around and locate my needs, fears, and hurt places, I understand myself better. I witness my vulnerability and am able to offer myself compassion. With this additional access to empathy, I don't pounce on myself as quickly. Instead, I practice my mothering skills—*Whoops, there's that rage popping up again. Let's see if I can give myself what I need.* By inviting my rage to tea, I am doing what I need most: I am mothering myself.

Maybe I can be precious too.

After identifying some of the underlying heartbeats of my rage—feeling disrespected, powerless, unconsidered, and unappreciated—I wanted to understand where they came from and why they are such tender spots for me.

I was sure rage burst into my life on the shoulders of motherhood. Most of the moms I interviewed said the same. But this isn't completely true, at least not for me. I think anger was bubbling under the surface of my skin for a long time. And motherhood has a knack for exposing the deepest recesses of ourselves.

Neurobiologist R. Douglas Fields, author of *Why We Snap: Understanding the Rage Circuit in Your Brain*, identifies stress as a significant factor of rage, and insult as a common trigger. We have all experienced insult and stress throughout our lives, but prior to having children many people haven't experienced the unceasing battering ram of stress that accompanies motherhood. Before motherhood, it's likely our rages were less frequent and even less intense. And because we were not mothers and were probably not screaming at children, we most likely did not fall into deep shame spirals afterward, wracked with self-hatred and guilt. These factors might make any pre-motherhood rage seem singular, brief, and less memorable.

When an event happens in our lives, the information is processed as two types of memories that travel down different pathways in our brains before they integrate into one memory. Explicit memories involve personal experience and information. It's the factual stuff we have to work to remember, like the name of an old elementary school classmate or the title of movie we saw years before. Implicit memories are unconscious and in the body. They are why we might involuntarily flinch when we hear clapping. Or cry at the smell of a certain kind of pipe tobacco. According to psychologist Jennifer Sweeton, "Implicit memories are the emotional responses and body sensations—this part doesn't have to do with fact, but feeling."

To access my own memories of pre-motherhood rage, I closed my eyes and appealed to my explicit memories by simply asking myself when I have raged before. Then I reached for implicit memories by trying to embody my rage. I imagined someone being unfair to me, and I let myself go all the way into that feeling. I tried to access feeling like I was going to explode, scream, or cry from frustration. I let my face get hot. I curled my fingers. All of these were attempts to give my body clues—sensations, emotions—so it knew what to look for as I let my mind flit around to my twenties, college, high school, summer camp, Hebrew school, childhood. It took me all of five minutes to locate my early rage. Once I discovered a memory, I walked around in it, like a museum of my life, trying to remember the context—who was there, which words were said. I stayed there until it was too much or I felt like I'd gotten all the information I could. Then I wrote down everything I could recall: a list of moments, people, feelings, words, rooms, sounds, and smells.

The first time I tried this, I closed my eyes and opened my mouth like I was going to scream. My hands turned into claws, and I stood there in a silent rage pose, letting my mind bring me to the place it associated with that feeling—my childhood home. I lived a happy childhood in a narrow, multistory row house in West Philadelphia. You could get from one end of the street to the other by hopping over the railing of all the connecting porches. In my rage memory, my mom was downstairs in the kitchen cooking. My father was probably reading a newspaper in the living room or taking a nap on the third floor in my parents' bedroom. I was on the second floor, playing a board game in the family room with my older brother, Alex.

Alex is one of those people with the supreme confidence nurtured in men. His sureness that he is right combined with a fat dollop of inflexibility made him somewhat of a dictator in our house growing up. Whether it was the TV shows we watched or the board games we played, he had the ability to bulldoze past every no until he got his yes.

Alex was a fierce competitor at domination board games like *Monopoly, Risk,* and *Axis & Allies.* I excelled at word games and *Memory.* (Perhaps this is why Alex is a successful business mogul and I record the details of my life. We all have our gifts!) In my memory, my brother had convinced me to play one of those domination games, and he wouldn't ease up or let me win. Despite our three-and-a-half-year age difference, Alex played ruthlessly, smiling broadly every time I landed on his properties teeming with hotels.

Every match was to the death, and I always died or became bankrupt—which is one and the same in a game about capitalism. When Alex threw down his tenth hotel in *Monopoly* or surrounded me with his formidable army as I held on for dear life to Yakutsk, my last uncolonized territory in *Risk,* seven-year-old me was helpless and angry. My demise felt designed.

In my memory, Alex had defeated me as usual, and I saw myself leaving the game, screaming in frustration, "I hate you!"

Alex just shrugged, palms up, "That's how you play the game."

Technically Alex was right. That *is* how you play the game, most games, actually, including life—the lived experience and the board game—that are designed by men for men, in which one player wins *because* of the subjugation, bankruptcy, or demise of the other players. *Risk* and *Axis & Allies?* Also designed by (white) men.

Monopoly was modeled after *The Landlord's Game,* created by Elizabeth Magie. In *The Landlord's Game,* there were two ways to play: the monopolist way, in which the players amass as much money and property as possible and win only when the other players have lost everything. Or the anti-monopolist way, in which all players benefit from another player's success. Magie's double-version game was meant as a primer (and warning) for kids about capitalism. It called attention to the designs already known. A man named Charles Darrow stole Magie's intellectual property and sold it to Parker Brothers, with only the monopolist rules. Darrow ended up a millionaire with a royalty agreement. Magie was later paid a mere five hundred dollars by Parker Brothers for her patent. Though Darrow and Parker Brothers did not act justly, they technically played by the rules and won at the game of capitalism, which was drafted by white men for more white men to win.

Because my brother was older, bigger, and played by the rules, I felt powerless. I walked away raging, but also unsure if I was overreacting. I didn't understand then that this feeling of my experience being denied or illegitimate is a direct result of playing a game with rules that were designed for me to fail. Similarly, mothering today is a no-win game, because the culture's rules of Motherhood weren't made by us or for us, despite what the PR team would have us believe.

In my next pre-motherhood rage memory, I was sitting on the edge of a queen-size mattress that lay on the floor in the center of the bedroom where I slept with my first live-in boyfriend. I was a senior in college. We shared the apartment with two other friends from Jewish summer camp. I was on the phone with the customer service department of my cell phone carrier, arguing over a mistaken thirty-five-dollar charge on my bill. The customer service representative kept telling me the call was made from my phone number. This was in 2002, well before WhatsApp and free international phone calls, before banks would just click a button and reimburse your account if your credit card was stolen.

"I don't even know anyone in France," I explained.

"Yes, ma'am. I understand. It says here the call was made at four fifteen a.m. to Grenoble on March seventeenth."

"Right, but see how crazy that is? I'm asleep at four fifteen. I don't know a single person in all of Europe!"

"Mmmhmm, I see."

"I need you to take that charge off."

"I'm not authorized to do that."

"Well, send me to someone who is, because I didn't make that call!"

Another agent. Another broken record. I started to feel like I was in a sci-fi movie. When agent number two told me he was going to transfer me, I screamed, "Do not transfer me!"

"Ma'am?"

"NOBODY IS LISTENING TO ME!"

My voice broke and tears came. My boyfriend, who was five years older, walked in and gently took the phone from me. I acquiesced and made for the door, then turned back to him and shouted loud enough for the customer service representative to hear:

"If they don't take that charge off, I'm switching to AT&T!"

My boyfriend put his hand up. *Enough.* I stood in the doorway of our bedroom watching. He spoke to the customer service representative calmly, almost jovially. He chuckled. *Chuckled!* My boyfriend looked up at me and winked. *I got this.* I stalked out of the room, grateful to escape customer service hell. But more than that, I could not stand to watch my boyfriend's complicity in this "Let's just work this out like men" moment. I could not bear to witness my boyfriend step into the rational man role, rescuing me from the hysterical woman role I felt cornered into.

I could have stopped it. I could have grabbed the phone and hung up. I could have yelled, "I won't play by your rules!" Or more likely, "FUCK YOU!" But I'm not sure who I would have been screaming at—the customer service guy who refused to believe me, or my boyfriend, who by helping me in this way was betraying me. I didn't yell at either of them. Would they have heard me if I had? I was invisible, cordoned off to my ineffectual woman island. I felt powerless, alone, and dismissed, which are some of the prominent, tender feelings that live underneath my rage.

Mining our early rages for information is critical because they commonly contain what I call rage triggers. In psychology, the word *trigger* is used to mean some kind of stimulus that brings on a post-traumatic stress disorder (PTSD) response, which may include remembering or reexperiencing past trauma. We often hear *trigger* used in reference to addiction. High school friends, a bar, or time with family can all trigger an addict to use again. When I use the word *trigger* in relation to mom rage, I'm referring to a psychological provocation—a tone of voice, a smell, a place, a person, a feeling—that produces a physiological response that's hard to control. This response happens because the trigger ignites the amygdalae.

Our two amygdalae, located deep in the temporal lobes on either side of the brain, play a primary role in decision-making and processing emotions and memory. The amygdalae are sometimes referred to as the brain's alarm system. When stress is mild, the brain's frontal lobes help us respond rationally and appropriately. But when stress is high or repetitive enough to make us feel intense anger, anxiety, fear, or aggression, the amygdalae can take over, igniting a fight, flight, or freeze response. Daniel Goleman calls this extreme response to stress an "amygdala hijack." It often results in a swift, irrational reaction, like rage, that we may regret later.

The igniting of the amygdalae is not necessarily a trauma response. Mom rage and its triggers can stem from high-stress situations without a trauma component. But when a mother is on the hunt for information about her rage, she shouldn't rule out trauma as a potential factor. There are two types of trauma, which Paul calls "Big T" and "little t" in his psychiatry practice.

Big-T trauma is an acute, possibly violent, incident, such as assault, abandonment by a guardian, or violation during childbirth. Twenty percent of women are victims of (reported) rape, 50 percent of women experience at least one traumatic event in their lifetime, and women are two to three times more likely than men to develop PTSD. Little-t trauma is a damaging psychological exposure that is not life-threatening but leaves a mark. Usually it's something repetitive you can't escape, often from within your family of origin. The repetitive exposure to being oppressed—feeling unsafe every day, experiencing daily microaggressions as a person of color or as a woman—can have traumatic impact. While little-t trauma is not the same as Big-T trauma, they both cause psychological harm and can lead to mom rage.

Patriarchy inherently lends itself to inflicting trauma. To live as a girl, to walk through the world every day as a woman, is to experience regular aggravations and repetitive stress that are worsened by the daily trauma of patriarchy and its henchmen: racism, homophobia, colonialism, transphobia, Islamophobia, ableism, etc. Women are told in a thousand ways that we are not valued and do not have power, and the little value and power we do have reside in our youth, our breasts, our asses, our legs—but only if they are a certain color and shape, adorned in certain clothing. Once we have used our bodies' power for their ultimate purpose of providing men pleasure and having babies, and our bodies are no longer the same, our value and power shrink to the realm of the home. Our remaining value is our ability to raise our children "right," keep them safe, keep a clean home, and stay on top of the family's social calendar, vacations, and meal planning. And don't forget take care of our spouses.

In the limited realm of home, where mothers are allowed to be "in charge," our power is warped to mean all the work with none of the support. When we inevitably have moments of feeling power*less* in the one domain the PR team tells us we should feel power*ful*, it is frightening, disappointing, stressful, insulting, and, unsurprisingly, infuriating.

In Ou and Hall's review of postpartum depression and anger studies, they found that feeling powerless is a key contributor to anger. The researchers identified three conditions associated with feeling powerless and angry: economic hardship, feeling trapped in current circumstances, and relationship conflict, including abuse, violence, infidelity, rejection, lack of support, and not feeling taken care of. Every mother I know experiences at least one of these conditions.

My pre-motherhood rage memories revealed that my rage triggers are connected to patriarchy and feeling powerless. With this new understanding, I can look at situations where I've raged, and see my triggers glaring brightly.

When Ollie asks me if he can do something and I say no, then Paul, who overhears our conversation, hollers from the other room, "I think it's okay."

I feel angry that Paul seems to think his answer is more right than mine. Or that it's okay to overturn mine, which he makes inevitable by saying it loud enough for Ollie to hear. This makes me feel powerless and disrespected. With one brief sentence, Paul has positioned me as Mean Mommy, while he gets to be Fun Dad: a common, gendered parenting trope, stemming from mothers being pushed into the primary parent role, always holding the un-fun responsibilities of parenting, like the schedule. When Paul does this, I also feel that we are not on a team together in our parenting.

*When Mae whines at Ollie, instead of using her
strong voice and her clear words to tell him
she doesn't like something he is doing.*

I'm triggered by Mae not using her strength to make her boundaries clear to her brother, and instead becoming a smaller entity. I feel fearful and angry that despite having me as a strong, feminist mother, at four years old the patriarchy has already taught her to shrink when her brother is domineering instead of embodying her power. My childhood dynamic with my own brother is certainly in play as well.

*When Paul comes home and, instead of
connecting with me, begins tidying the house that
I pre-tidied in anticipation of his arrival.*

When the first thing Paul engages with upon entering our home is the clutter, I feel that he doesn't see all the effort I put into making the house nice. I feel like my labor and my whole self—since my identity is intertwined with the constant work of mothering—are invisible to Paul, which makes me feel devalued and unseen.

*When I've worked hard on dinner, and Ollie comes into the
kitchen and asks, "What are we having for dinner?"*

"Turkey meatloaf."
"What else?"
"Broccoli."
"What else?"
"Oranges."
"What else?" (ad infinitum)

I feel that my labor is unappreciated by Ollie. Making food is loaded for me both because of a mother's stereotypical role as the home chef, and because of how much time and effort I put into the week's food planning, buying, and cooking to ensure, despite his extremely rigid sensory issues around food, that Ollie is healthy and fed.

———

Everyone experiencing mom rage has their own individual triggers. Carrie, the social worker who lives in Sacramento with her wife, Ameena, and their two young sons, identifies yelling as one of her prime rage triggers. She doesn't have to close her eyes and go down memory lane to discover it. Carrie grew up in a home with a mother with mental illness, who yelled constantly.

Having yelling as a rage trigger is particularly tricky, because in addition to the kids "screaming at the top of their lungs when they tantrum," Ameena also has mom rage and often expresses it through yelling. When Ameena yells, Carrie has to work to remind herself, "Okay, Ameena is angry. She's not my mom saying crazy things." When the kids yell, Carrie says she feels powerless. "It's kind of traumatizing to me, even though I know they're obviously not my mother." The yelling ignites Carrie's amygdalae: "I'm either gonna fight my kids or I want to run away from them."

Ameena experiences a mix of fight, flight, and freeze responses when she gets triggered. Carrie says, "Ameena will yell, 'I'm done with you!'" and then flee the room. Sometimes, especially when the younger child bites and hits Ameena, "She will just start crying. She'll crumple and kind of fall into a puddle, and not fight back." This is how the freeze response can look during mom rage.

By engaging with her rage instead of pushing it aside, Carrie has been able to pinpoint some of the patterns and needs that underpin it. She notices that she rages more at night when she's tired and irritable. She's quicker to rage when there is a time crunch, especially when she feels like she has a million things to do and her kids aren't moving fast enough. Carrie's mom rage gets triggered when she feels abandoned by Ameena, left to trudge through the hard parts of parenting by herself. "When we're running late to school and my partner slept late, when I feel like I'm doing it all alone—the lunches, the socks and shoes, the sunscreen, driving them to school—that's where [the rage] comes out."

Understanding our triggers can help prevent mom rage. While the fight-flight-freeze stress response is involuntary, learning the ins and outs of our rage triggers provides us with self-awareness. The more mindful we are of our triggers—our wounded or hurt places—the more likely we'll be able to recognize that the trigger is in play when we start to feel ourselves getting provoked into that familiar rage state. Eventually, with practice and support, we may be able to attend to that pulsing hurt place *before* the amygdalae get activated.

Mindfulness practices, like meditation, have been proven to reduce stress and make the amygdalae less reactive to stimuli. There is research that my own mindfulness practice of journaling has a calming effect, and helps with depression, stress, and anxiety. Writing helps me to understand all the parts of myself, including the angry parts. Once we become cognizant of the life experiences that have become triggers, mindfulness can help us slow down enough to notice we are getting triggered and stop ourselves from flying into a rage.

Though I did much of the work of inviting my rage to tea through journaling, I wasn't really on my own. In addition to Nat, I had a couples therapist, an anger management group for mothers, and sessions with my life coach Fran. Inviting my rage to tea required deep and continuous self-investigation with the support of multiple professionals.

Because Carrie knows her yelling trigger's origin, she is sometimes able to recognize it mid-rage and stop herself. "There are times my rage comes out with a level of yelling where I can see my mother in the back of my mind doing that same yelling, and I'll think, 'I know this isn't good for [my kids]. They need me to stay calm.'" But she and Ameena have also called upon outside support to help them deal with their mom rage. Carrie described a couples therapist who once talked to her and Ameena about the importance of them not solving their kids' problems for them, and instead reflecting back what they hear their kids are experiencing. The therapist suggested they help their sons name their emotions, and then the moms can empathize with those emotions. Carrie said when she remembers to do this, it slows everything down and she's able access empathy for her kids. "Then I'm in their experience, and I'm not in mine as much. When I'm in an emotional experience of someone else, that helps me not go from zero to a hundred."

When Carrie does not have the presence of mind to step into her children's emotional experience, she employs other strategies. Sometimes she turns on music to "mentally go somewhere else." If she catches herself being sarcastic to the kids, she'll try and talk herself down like an "inner cheerleader," saying things like, "This isn't gonna go the way you want it to." Other times, Carrie will try to interrupt her rage cycle by picturing a particularly terrible rage she's had. "There have been a couple times when I've flown into a rage, and my children have run to their beds and gotten under their covers. Those times felt awful. So that inner cheerleader is trying to visualize it and warn me, 'That's what could happen. You don't want that.'"

I love the empathetic voice Carrie uses when her inner cheerleader speaks to her rage. Inviting our rage to tea is like exercising a muscle. The more we do it, the more easily we can treat our rage like a friend, offering a listening ear or advice, or even a loving warning, as Carrie describes.

Inviting my own rage to tea has helped me access empathy for myself, and in turn for my kids. Maybe empathy is a practice too. Sometimes I'm able to slow my triggered self down enough that I can find my empathy before it's too late.

Let's return to the dreaded daily double—toothbrushing. But this time, because of the work I've done inviting my rage to tea, the outcome does not end in rage:

Ollie (age seven) and Mae (age three) are in the bathroom together during toothbrushing time. I choose to take care of myself by not standing in there hovering. I tell myself I'm going to let them brush. Or play around for a couple minutes. However they use that time is on them, and I won't interject. Then I'll take a turn brushing each of their teeth and be done with it. As much as I need a break from their messing around during toothbrushing, I'm pretty sure my kids need a break from me being on top of them to do the task "right." (Again, is this my perfectionism or am I teaching executive functioning? We all need a break either way.)

After a minute or two, I walk toward the bathroom and see Mae in the doorway, trying to push the ajar door all the way open. She is grunting because despite Ollie having been told a hundred times not to push back against doors people are trying to open, he is using his body's force to close it. He has his reasons for wanting the door closed. It is also a bit of a game for him. I stretch my arm out in front of me as I rush to the door and bellow, "Stop pushing the door!" At the same moment the words are leaving my mouth, and before my hand makes contact with the door, Ollie gives one hard push, and Mae careens backward, knocking her head against a rectangular metal piece that juts out from the door frame.

Mae falls to the floor clutching her head. She can barely catch her breath, and is doing that terrible silent scream where the snot and spit are coming out in strings, but the voice is caught. When her screams erupt, my stomach leaps. I feel every cell of my animal body respond to Mae's howls. I fall to the hall floor just outside the bathroom, and pull her into my lap, clutching her body as I rock her and check her head for blood. When I find none, I feel my deep fear release, making way for the fury rising inside my chest. I look up at Ollie standing in the bathroom doorway, quietly watching.

On the edge of explosion, I take in his face, searching to see if he understands what he's done and if he feels anything. I recognize regret and sadness in his wet, almond eyes, mirror images of mine. I take a slow breath and see that his heart is just like my heart—full of self-punishment. I open my arms to him and say no words at all. Their two heads nestled in my neck, the three of us rock until our breathing drops into a single, even rhythm.

Because I was able to slow myself down enough to wonder what Ollie was feeling, I saw his shame, his momentary sureness that he was not good. And I felt the sting of recognition. Once I registered that he was having those feelings, I was able to step out of my experience and into his, offering empathy and compassion, and the forgiveness he might not have been able to give himself.

The goal of inviting our rage to tea is to give ourselves greater awareness of when we're feeling triggered and what's causing it. This helps us to recognize when we're in the Ramp-Up and Whack-a-Mole phases of the Mom Rage Cycle. Before this reframing of our rage and the work of self-investigation, mom rage never felt like a choice we were making; it was automatic. Our new understanding of our triggers gives us the capability—when we are tunneling down the road toward the explosion of phase three—to slow ourselves down and make a conscious non-rage choice.

In the year after I had my three therapy appointments with Rachel, I was in a session with Nat, and I said something out loud that she suggested I write down. I kept those two sentences on a scrap of paper in my purse until it disintegrated years later. I must have reread those sentences two hundred times. Mindfulness and self-love come in many forms, and all of them need practice.

Ollie is a four-year-old boy, and he is good.

I am a thirty-five-year-old woman, and I am also good.

7 RESCUE YOUR PARTNER FROM ENEMY TERRITORY

Because nothing makes me happier and nothing
makes me sadder than you.

—Nicole Krauss, *The History of Love*

Sometimes I fantasize about being divorced.

I don't want the heartbreak or the meanness, the money fights or the bitterness. Even "amicable" divorces seem painful. Honestly, I don't even want to be divorced from Paul. I just really like the idea of parenting and being married every *other* week. A week on/week off custody arrangement. During Paul's week with the kids, I'd get a break. Not a grocery-store break. Not a texting-while-pooping break. Not even an exercise-and-brunch break. But a day-after-day-of-silence respite. A week-long reprieve from the constant need. A seven-day release from decision-making fatigue. An every-other-week vacation from preparing and navigating everyone's food preferences and issues all day long. An all-inclusive, comprehensive, surround-sound, motherfucking break!

During Ollie's toddler years, when Paul and I were fighting a lot, Ollie had become more challenging as two-year-olds are wont to do in their maniacal forward march toward personhood. His sensory-related needs were also beginning to surface. (No short sleeves! No meat, vegetables, cheese, or beans! No crowds!) I was learning to navigate Ollie's big feelings while trying to handle my own. On top of that, my resentment toward Paul was swelling. I felt he consistently undercut my authority. I was using all my reserves to deftly and calmly parent Ollie, and Paul's undermining felt like the final thread to my sanity. My rage zeroed in on him.

I noticed the longer I let little Ollie watch videos, the bigger his freak-out would be when I told him screen time was over. So instead of letting him watch for forty-five minutes, I learned to transition him to a new activity at twenty or thirty minutes. One Saturday afternoon, I walked into Ollie's room and told him it was time to close the laptop. Predictably, Ollie protested loudly and with tears (a low-level freak-out). From down the hall, Paul said, "It's only been thirty minutes. I think it's okay if he watches a little more." Having spotted a weakness, Ollie began to whine in earnest, "Pweeeeze!"

Unwittingly or not, Paul had wedged me into a corner. I could let Ollie continue watching and weather the toddler hurricane that would come after forty-five minutes of screen time. Or, I could be Mean Mommy and stick to my guns, enduring Ollie's giant freak-out, while Paul winced at Ollie's screams and shook his head at my rigidity. This sort of thing became such a trigger that the thousandth time it happened I shouted at Paul loud enough for the neighbors to hear, "NO ONE IS TALKING TO YOU!!!" Then I had to grovel for my inappropriate outburst.

Instead of being unified in raising our beloved, tiny tyrant, Paul's parenting avatar was sparring with mine, our different parenting strategies cheering and booing on opposite sides of the ring. Co-parenting was often harder than solo parenting. Weekends felt challenging to the point of dread. The eating and nap-time routines I'd implemented through an exhaustive process of trial and error were golden structures that helped me survive the long weekdays when I was in charge and Paul was at work. At best, Paul saw these routines as optional. He chalked up my frustration (which often presented as rage) to my being fearful and controlling. I felt I was having a legitimate reaction to the hard work of mothering while being unseen, unappreciated, and then undermined.

This misalignment between Paul's understanding of my rage and my own understanding of my rage is due to a slew of gender-related differences in how anger, motherhood, and fatherhood are perceived. Because dads don't experience the identity tumult of matrescence and rarely bear the weight of primary parenthood, they don't see or feel the stress mothers are under or the double amount of domestic labor mothers do. Dads are by-products of a culture that disapproves of women's anger, so dads tend to blame moms who rage instead of seeing the ways our anger is warranted. The differences in fatherhood and motherhood, and the gendered perceptions of anger, add to the gulf that often forms between men and women in parenting partnerships.

Divorce as a labor reprieve for mothers came up in a few of my interviews. One mom in a same-sex marriage said, "If I were a halftime parent, I would have a lot more bandwidth to stay calm and actively manage my kids." A single mom confirmed our yearning: "One great thing about being divorced is I get two days off a week."

When Frannie, a bisexual Taiwanese Canadian mom of two tweens, was married, she felt jealous of her divorced mom friends with split custody. "I was like, 'So hold on. For a whole week you get to turn off your brain to any responsibilities that have to do with the children?'" Frannie's husband worked eighty-hour weeks as a chef, so "all the child-rearing fell on me." Once they got divorced, Frannie felt a new freedom on the stretch of days her husband had the kids: "I was like, 'holy shit, I feel like a teenager. I can leave my dirty laundry on the ground or let the dishes pile up.'" Dirty dishes and piles of soiled laundry are not the real dream. They are just representations of that teenage sense of selfish freedom, a break from putting other people first. During her days off, Frannie gets to experience doing exactly what she wants to do when she wants to do it. She gets to be someone other than Mother again.

I know if I actually got divorced, I'd be bereft. Despite our parenting squabbles, Paul is my North Star. Still, it says something about the current state of Motherhood that moms who are still in love with our spouses and don't want to get divorced are dreaming about it. It is the only way of getting a break that we can imagine.

While we were never truly on the verge of divorce, my rage pushed Paul and me apart. Each of my rages was a brick of resentment. Paul's hurt and furious reaction was the mortar, spread thick. Eventually our collective pain forged a wall, the two of us isolated on opposite sides.

If I raged at Ollie, I didn't want to talk to Paul about it. It was too hard to speak my shame and regret out loud. There was no reprimand Paul could give me that I wasn't already giving myself with three times as much vitriol. In my armored shell of anguish, I was completely closed off to Paul, so he mostly left me alone. We'd be in the same room, oceans apart.

I felt deserted in my experience of rage, but also in my frustrations around parenting. Paul never talked about his challenges.

When Ollie was three, I said to Paul in couples therapy, "It's like you have no issues in parenting."

"Of course I do!" he responded.

"Then why don't you ever complain to me? Why don't you ever catch my gaze across the room and roll your eyes about the way our kid is acting?" Just the simple act of the two of us sharing an eye roll would bring a lightness to difficult parenting moments and make me feel connected to Paul.

"I don't want to roll my eyes about my kid," Paul responded, plunging me into the loneliness of bad-parent guilt. *It doesn't have to be like this*, I thought sadly. *We don't each have to hold the challenges of parenting alone, fingering them like shame stones hidden in our pockets.*

The example of Carrie and Ameena, who both have mom rage, shows that co-parents can come together instead of turning away from each other when parenting gets hard. "The gift of having a co-parent means that when Ameena is around, I can be like, 'I'm going to lose it,'" said Carrie. The couple's connection, or disconnection, is an important factor in their mom rage. When they're not getting along, Carrie said she doesn't have the internal resources to calmly handle their kids' tantrums. "But when we're in a good place, we can at least look at each other across the room and roll our eyes together. It gives me that little push I need to get through a moment."

When Ameena is in the Rage phase of the Mom Rage Cycle, Carrie sometimes takes her out of the room and says, "I'm trying to help you. You're gonna feel mad at yourself later for using anger like that." Sometimes it doesn't work, and Ameena responds, "Oh my gosh, you are coming between us. You're not supporting me in this!" But other times Ameena is able to hear Carrie and discontinue raging by resetting with more patience, or just remaining in a different room until she cools down.

Once the rage has been cut short, the couple sometimes provides an after-care postmortem for each other, discussing how to avoid rage the next time that trigger pops up. Carrie admits this doesn't usually work if the problem-solving is coming from the non-raging parent. The raging parent is tender in this moment and can easily feel judged, so they've figured out a few work-arounds:

- The non-raging parent opens up the conversation with empathy: "Yeah, I know it's hard."
- They use language previously agreed upon that doesn't feel triggering: "This is not good for our children; we don't want them to experience this on the daily."
- The couple "huddles," and discusses ideas for accountability so the interaction doesn't happen that same way again.

Carrie's use of the word "huddle" makes me think of a sports team. That team aspect seems to be key for both preventing rage in the first place, and for avoiding an isolating shame spiral if rage does rear its head. Being on the same team is exactly what I'm after when I yearn for a shared eye roll across the room. I've tried to bring Paul into my rage process the way Carrie and Ameena are entwined in each other's. We discussed the idea of him taking over when I'm heading toward rage, but I'm not always quick enough, or mindful enough, to beat the rage explosion in time to say, "I need you to tag in!" When Paul has tried to initiate taking over without me asking, it often escalates me further, because I feel that only my fury is being acknowledged, not the legitimacy of my frustration. Instead of validation or connection or support, I feel judgment. I don't envy Paul in this situation. Aborting someone's rage is a dangerous and delicate task, like flossing a tiger.

Maggie, the mom of twins who does listening circles with her family, used couples therapy to troubleshoot with her husband about how he can help make her aware of her rising anger before she hits a boiling point. Their counselor suggested they think of a phrase Maggie's husband can say. At the time, their girls were watching a lot of *Daniel Tiger*. The couple decided Maggie's husband would say a line from a song from the show, "Take a deep breath, and let it go." But when they tried it, Maggie would hit that same wall of indignation that Carrie, Ameena, and I often hit when our partners try to stop our rages. "I'd get even more enraged, because I'd feel like, 'Are you saying that I'm acting crazy?'"

Eventually, Maggie and her husband found a phrase that worked while watching the movie *Monsters, Inc.* with their daughters. Maggie had seen the movie before, but this was her first time viewing it as a parent. The twins got scared at a scene near the end, in which Sully, a sweet monster whose job is to scare children until they scream, roars loudly, terrifying the little girl he's befriended named Boo. Afterward, Sully sees photos that captured him when he was mid-roar, and for the first time, he sees himself as the terrifying monster Boo saw.

While watching, Maggie had an emotional realization: "Boo is my little girls, and I'm Sully. To them, I must look like this big, scary monster." Maggie asked her husband to say "Sully" when he notices she's losing control. "It helps me remember I'm hitting that monster level. I don't mean it in a negative way. I think of Sully as this really sweet character." Because Maggie has tender feelings for Sully and sees him as a complex character—both monstrous *and* loving—the word *Sully* doesn't feel judgmental when her husband uses it, so Maggie is able to take it in without escalating further.

Eventually, I, too, found my version of Sully. But first I found despair.

Over the years, I've had a few "I must fix the rage!" moments of desperation. Each time, I tried a new potential solution: talk therapy, medication, running, a twelve-week anger management group, couples therapy. Some work better than others. None are a magical snap-your-fingers solution.

In June 2020, three months into full-time parenting with no school or childcare whatsoever and no end to the COVID-19 pandemic in sight, I hit another wall of desperation. I was beside myself—exhausted, livid, afraid. How long would our country expect mothers to put our entire selves aside to pick up the childcare slack? With no parenting breaks, no opportunities for emotional support from friends other than texting, and very little time for writing, I felt out of control. It felt like being thrown back into those early years of matrescence when my time and body did not belong to me, and my only purpose was the care of my children. All attempts at self-determination were futile, and voicing my misery felt almost unpatriotic. We were all sacrificing, weren't we? People were dying, for god's sake. Paul, who was also either working or parenting with no breaks, had even less bandwidth than usual for my despair. I had to hold it together.

I began reading Ronald Potter-Efron's *Rage: A Step-by-Step Guide to Overcoming Explosive Anger*. I was excited and horrified to recognize myself in his descriptions of the different types of rage people struggle with. It was like taking a personality quiz in *Teen Magazine*, except with much more gravity. The discussion of impotent rage, which stews and simmers over time, read to me like a dark definition of motherhood, especially pandemic motherhood: "Impotent rage is a feeling of tremendous fury that is triggered by the sense of helplessness that occurs when a person is unable to control important situations. Ragers feel helpless to change the situation after they've made repeated efforts."

I also recognized myself in the description of the shame-based rager. When Potter-Efron asks, "Do you become irate when people seem to be ignoring you?" I responded with a resounding *yes*!

My horror kicked in when I read the following: "The shame-rage message is scary: 'You are shaming me. What you are saying makes me feel weak and powerless. I am humiliated. It feels like you are trying to destroy me. I can't let that happen. Instead . . . I have to shame you. I might even have to destroy you.'"

Terrified I might be a shame-based rager, I sobbed on the phone to Nat as I walked. (During the pandemic, I opted for audio instead of video therapy so I could multitask and get in a single weekly walk by myself.)

"I think I do try to shame Ollie! When he's doing something over and over that makes me crazy, I don't say 'What's wrong with you?' but in some ways I am giving him that message. I am afraid I'm messing him up forever!"

"Does the book give advice on what to do?"

"It says to gather a support system to help you stop. But my whole support system is you and my mom friends I text. I can't use Paul."

[*Typical therapy pause . . .*]

"Do you think there's a way you can use Paul as an ally?"

"Like how?"

"Well, besides you, he's the adult who knows your rage best, right?"

"Yeah, I guess so."

"So maybe he has information. Maybe he can help you."

I had never considered that Paul could be a companion along my rage journey, rather than an enemy. If I wasn't angry with him, I was feeling isolated, ashamed, and judged by him. But maybe Nat was right. I'm not able to observe myself when I'm about to spew fire or when I'm mid-rage. Partners are in the unique position of being able to witness mothers' rages when we aren't capable of witnessing ourselves. I decided to take a leap and ask Paul for help.

One night, lying on our bed, I turn to look at Paul. He's propped up on pillows next to me, his laptop resting on his stretched-out legs. He is long and lean in his skinny jeans and flannel plaid button-up, unaware of himself, as he snorts with laughter at Snoop Dogg's YouTube talk show *GGN* (Double G News Network). His earbuds are pressed in tight, and above them his rolled-up, red beanie covers his shaved head. Since the pandemic began, we've spent countless evenings like this—lying next to each other staring at our separate laptops. It is as close to being alone as we can access. Watching Paul's eyes get wet from laughing so hard, I hate to pull him out of his Snoop world. I am afraid he'll look annoyed if I ask for his attention, and really be annoyed when I tell him what I want to talk about. I take a breath for bravery and tap him. Paul pauses the video, turning to me, his thick, Groucho Marx eyebrows aloft, the remnants of a smile still on his lips.

"What's up?"

"I have a question. Can you take a quick break from your show?"

"Sure," he says, pulling his earbuds out.

"I read somewhere that people usually have physical tells that they are about to rage or are in a rage. It could be pressing my fingers to my eyes, looking up at the ceiling, a loud, prolonged sigh, wringing my hands . . . something like that. Have you ever noticed anything like that?"

"No, not really," Paul replies, a little too quickly. Rage talk is not what he wanted to take a break from Snoop for. I take a slow breath, trying to stay upbeat for the favor I'm about to request.

"Would you be open to trying to observe me to see if you notice any? If we can figure out what my tells are, it might help me to stop a rage before it starts." Talking about my rage with Paul always feels dangerous because it's not a neutral topic—we both have big feelings about it. But since we're in a calm moment, and I am not asking Paul for comfort he might not want to give, this vulnerable ask feels a little less scary.

"Okay," agrees Paul, glancing at his screen.

"I know that one of my tells is clapping," I continue hastily before I lose him, "but I think by time I start clapping, it's probably too late. I'm already mid-rage." Paul nods. I forge ahead. "Well, once we figure out what my tells are, can you say to me, 'Are you in the yellow zone?'"

Paul and I learned about "the zones of regulation" from an occupational therapist when Ollie was first diagnosed with sensory processing disorder. Certain colors stand for groups of emotions. Saying "I'm in the red zone" (angry, out of control, devastated, terrified) was an accessible way for Ollie to identify an intense emotional state. Yellow stood for *some* loss of control (anxiety, silliness, frustration). I figured if the zones of regulation were useful for Ollie at age five, why not for me at thirty-nine? Just like Maggie has a sweet connotation for Sully, I have tender feelings for "Are you in the yellow zone?" It makes me think of teaching Ollie that all his feelings are valid, we just have to be aware of them. Plus, because it's a phrase Ollie understands, if Paul says it in front of him, not only is it good modeling, but it normalizes both of our struggles. Everyone gets in the yellow zone sometimes.

"I can try," Paul answers.

"Okay, thank you. I really appreciate it." Paul puts his earbuds back in and returns to his happy place with Snoop.

I suspect most partners, including Paul, want to help the moms they love with their fury but don't know how. Engaging with one's partner's rage might feel like walking into a booby-trapped room. When I rage, Paul's instinct is to retreat, to run in the opposite direction from my pursuing anger. By asking him to observe me, I am essentially asking Paul to watch me rev up, brace himself for impact, and then, regardless of his emotional reaction, stay put and take copious mental notes.

The very next night, our joint investigation into my physical rage tells bore fruit. After putting the kids to bed, Paul and I, reclined on our bed, are discussing what we should do with the advance money I'm going to get for writing this book. It'll be the first real chunk of change I'll have earned in years. I tell Paul that I want to put the money toward a down payment on a house. Living in the San Francisco Bay Area has meant that, as a single-earner household, we have not been able to enter the housing market. During the pandemic, with the four of us at home all the time, the walls of our own two-bedroom, one-bathroom rental have felt like they are caving in on us. I dream of a grassy backyard. And a second toilet.

Paul already knows I want a bigger place and a house of our own. He'd like that, too, but given the ridiculousness of the local housing market, he is perfectly content to stay where we are and to be lifelong renters. He launches into an explanation of why using the money for a house is not a good idea. It is wiser, he insists, to put the money into our children's college funds. Paul is good at sounding firm and clear, using declarative phrases like "It is a better financial choice to" and "It doesn't make any sense to."

When he finishes talking, I begin to reply. I want to say to Paul that just because he's decided what we should do with the advance money doesn't mean that's the final decision for our family. *I earned that money*, I think to myself. *I should have a say! Maybe I will allow him to put a chunk of it in the kids' college funds.* When my words arrive, they come out labored, as if I am working hard to form and eject the sounds. My voice drops an octave. Propped up on the elbow of one arm, the tips of my fingers on my other hand come together into a duck bill. My duck hand shoots out in front of me, moving slightly with each word.

"I. Will. *Allow.* You . . ."

Paul puts his hand up. "Are you in the yellow zone?"

I pause. *Am I?* I take notice of the stilted way I'm speaking, and realize I am talking like that because I'm playing a losing game of whack-a-mole with my anger, working so hard not to scream, *It's* my *money! How dare you try to tell me what to do with my money!* Never mind that Paul has never once made me feel like the money he earns isn't equally mine. I am not thinking rationally, because I am already triggered, zooming full steam ahead on the train to rage. I can't believe I didn't notice.

I've already done the work of inviting my rage to tea, but never in the middle of a rage episode. I remember that rage covers up more vulnerable emotions, like sadness, shame, and fear, so I close my eyes right there on the bed in front of Paul, who watches silently. *Where does it hurt?* I ask myself. *What are you afraid of?* My mind scans for wounds, and immediately finds them, pulsing red.

As usual, patriarchy and powerlessness are at the top of my pain heap. I have been earning money since I was thirteen and financially supporting myself since I was twenty-one. Relying on Paul as our family's primary financial earner is not entirely comfortable for me, even though I chose it and benefit from the privilege it grants me to be an artist and do the work that got me to this place of some financial success. I keep scanning. I hit on my fear that not only will we never buy a house, but that I have no control over what we do with our money. Paul and I can both be very intense about what we think is right, and I sometimes feel powerless when Paul sets his mind on how certain things should be. I started to feel like our conversation was going in a paternalistic direction—less like a brainstorm and more like a decree. The patriarchal history of fathers controlling their families' wealth, one of the many ways men have wielded control over women's freedom, lives in my mom rage basement and informs my triggers. I had seen the real-life consequences of these gendered power dynamics around money, particularly when couples get divorced, and the non-earning parent (so often a mother) has to fight to have her labor in the home recognized and quantified.

When Paul spoke so definitively about not using my book advance money to buy a house, it was like watching the soft, sun-bellied center of my over-easy fantasy slide right into the compost. My eyes still closed, I focus my self-scan on that sadness and fear, and my grief rises up like steam. I burst into chest-heaving sobs. My bodily reaction is faster than my own cognition. The quick shift from almost rage to involuntary weeping surprises us both. Paul wraps me up in his arms and holds me until I am ready to talk.

By rescuing my partner from the "he doesn't understand" island I'd placed him on years before, I felt safe enough to show him my sadness, shame, and fear—emotions that don't exhibit threat or ignite his own fight-or-flight impulse. That night, we talked until we understood each other.

After my emotional outpouring I was awash with relief. We discovered what my physical tells are: my voice gets deeper, my enunciation sharpens to a fine point, and my hands gesticulate with the cadence of my slowed down speech. This exercise helped us recognize when I'm triggered and interrupt my rage cycle. When I enlisted Paul as an ally—a co-conspirator—we were able to finally step toward each other.

The distance between us did not completely disappear, however. There was still the task of getting Paul to understand mom rage as more than me having an anger problem. Partners, fathers in particular, tend to think their wives' fury is the same as their own. Whenever I publish or talk about mom rage, fathers ask me, "What about dad rage?" If dads think their rage is on the same plane as mom rage, then the question they're really wondering is: "If I can control my anger, why can't she?" This comparison makes mothers feel more unseen in their experience of mom rage, and leaves fathers feeling mystified and unempathetic.

On the one hand, these dads who assume there must be equivalent dad rage have a point. Raising children is a job that can bring anyone to their knees. Amidst all their sweetness, their enthusiastic curiosity, and the funny things they say, children are gorgeous little dictators who require a never-ending supply of patience. Exploding at various points on the decades-long parenting journey is more of a *when* than an *if*, regardless of whether the caregiver identifies as a mother, father, baba, or any other moniker. Emotions don't discriminate based on gender or sex.

But while anyone can experience rage, dads need to understand that moms and dads are not raging on the same playing field. One key difference is that for most women and femme people, anger is viewed as ugly and out of control. Angry femmes are treated as hysterical and bitchy. Angry men and masculine people, on the other hand, are much more likely to be seen as assertive and in charge. Their anger is interpreted as a sign of alpha positioning.

In the study mentioned earlier, in which participants viewed angry men in the workplace as having higher status and angry women as having lower status, the participants also linked women's anger to their personality. A woman's anger was seen as a character flaw—she is bitter, shrill, aggressive. But men's anger was dismissed by study participants as situational. They thought the men yelled because no one was listening, not because the men were impatient. There was an external and therefore understandable reason for the men's anger. Men's fury—particularly middle- and upper-class white men's fury—is socially forgiven and often rewarded. Women's anger being blamed on their character is especially likely for Black women, whose anger is deemed invalid based on gender and worthy of punishment based on race.

While our perceptions of anger are greatly influenced by race, class, and culture, we learn from Motherhood's PR team (which, lest we forget, is the mouthpiece of the white supremacist capitalist heterosexist patriarchy) that a dad's rage, particularly a white dad's rage, is unremarkable. If a white man's anger is stigmatized at all, it's only if his behavior is abusive. The anger of a woman of any race is stigmatized regardless of whether it's abusive. And dads yelling? Well, that's not a bad dad, that's the alpha getting the kids in line. But when moms rage, the PR team tells us she has "left her station" and gone against everything mothers are supposed to be. As a result, moms are more likely to fall into a shame spiral. *What have I done? What kind of a mother am I!* Fathers, meanwhile, tend to feel vindicated in their anger. Even if they feel bad about having yelled, their behavior doesn't call their identity and worth into question in the way it does for mothers. In 1998, psychologist Ann M. Kring from the University of California, Berkeley, reviewed studies on gender and anger that showed men and women self-report anger episodes with similar frequency, but that women experience much more shame.

Cheryl, the civil rights lawyer from Rockville, Maryland, who internalizes her rage, described her husband as "super ragey" toward their son. He yells, stomps, slams doors, and even once punched a hole in a wall. When his rage is through, he does not go down a shame spiral. Instead, Cheryl said, "He screams, and then he's mad at you for making him scream. He feels justified." And though Cheryl's husband apologizes, he does what Cheryl called "the man apology": "He hasn't even finished saying 'I'm sorry,' and he's already telling the person what they did to make him mad, like, 'I'm sorry I yelled, but you have to understand that you can't . . .'" Not only do *other* people forgive men's anger by thinking it's situational or someone else's fault, men forgive their own anger for the same reasons.

Paul has his moments with our kids, and even with me, when his voice rises to a decibel level that makes us cower. At eight years old, Ollie started wearing Invisalign, two removable clear retainers made from a mold of Ollie's teeth. Each week, Ollie would switch to a new set that was slightly different from the one before it. And over many months, his teeth shifted to give the last few grown-up teeth more room to come in.

The problem was that one of the retainers kept breaking before it was time for the next one, requiring us to accelerate the replacement schedule. It happened over and over, eventually causing us to jump weeks ahead. The entire system was getting thrown out of whack, and we kept having to return to the orthodontist's office. Though the continual breaking of Ollie's lower Invisalign ended up being the fault of the mold, Paul blamed Ollie. To be fair, I also assumed Ollie must be doing something that was causing the retainer to break. But interestingly, I didn't get heated about this, probably for the same reason Paul *did* get triggered—Paul was the parent in charge of all things orthodontia. He took Ollie to all his appointments. He called the orthodontist when the retainers broke. He made sure the Invisalign case always made its way into Ollie's lunch box in the mornings, and that it always came home with us from other people's houses. As the person who handled the communication, scheduling, responsibility, and the invisible labor of always knowing where it was and where it needed to be, Paul was the primary parent for Ollie's Invisalign, and as a result had primary parent emotions about it.

One night, as Ollie was getting into bed, he revealed to Paul that his Invisalign had broken yet again. Paul went ballistic, screaming, "What's wrong with you?" I am no saint when it comes to saying things I shouldn't, but this particular phrase hits me as an unfair dig at someone's core. It feels specifically off limits to say to Ollie because he's neurodivergent. Isn't that a message the world will give him throughout his life because he does certain things differently from other people? When Paul says it to our kids, especially to Ollie, I get scared it'll latch on to their psyches and follow them around their whole lives. Eventually, as Paul continued his tirade, Ollie burst into tears.

Paul left the room, and I went to Ollie, who was weeping in his bed.

"Did you know I used to have retainers, just like your Invisalign, when I was a kid, older than you even?"

"Really?" he asked, his sobs pausing.

"Really. And I lost them a lot. I threw them away with my lunch bag at school so many times. Once I even dug through a pile of trash until I found the brown paper lunch bag with my name on it, because Grandma and Grandpa told me that if I lost them again, I'd have to pay a hundred dollars from my saved allowance money."

Ollie's eyes widened. "Did you lose them again?"

"I did. And I paid that hundred dollars. And Grandma and Grandpa were so mad, but I was even more mad at myself. You and I have that in common. We have to forgive ourselves when we mess up. You are good even when you make mistakes. You'll try not to break them again, right?"

Ollie nodded.

"So that's all you can do." I kissed him goodnight and he went to sleep.

The next day, Ollie came home from school and showed me that his replacement Invisalign had broken in less than twenty-four hours.

"Don't tell Daddy," he begged.

"We have to tell Daddy, but I'm going to talk to him. He's not going to get mad this time."

I went to Paul and told him what happened, and explained that Ollie needed him not to blow up, that nothing Paul could say was worse than what Ollie was saying to himself, and that he couldn't really take it emotionally if Paul flew off the handle again. Paul agreed. He talked gently to Ollie about it briefly. The next day Paul took Ollie to get a new mold of his teeth taken. The bottom Invisalign rarely broke after that.

The difference between my rage and Paul's is that when the yelling incident is over, Paul's anguish is also complete. Sure, he feels bad that he yelled and apologizes. But because Paul was raised to be a man, his anger doesn't threaten his sense of legitimacy and goodness as a person or father. He doesn't think, *Gee, my behavior was totally out of control. What's wrong with me?* Because I was raised with the same cultural messaging around gender and anger, I also don't fault Paul for his rage. I do just what the participants in the study did—absolve Paul of his rage by hanging the blame on external forces. (*The kids* were *being pretty disrespectful.*) I, on the other hand, view my rage as a character flaw. When I rage the same way Paul did, it can take days for me to get over it and forgive myself.

In addition to the gender imbalance of societal perceptions of anger, dads partnered to women also need to consider that because they are not usually the primary parent, the cultural expectations for them are drastically lower than they are for mothers. Motherhood is touted as the top of the mountain for women, "the best job in the world." With that kind of pressure to not only become mothers, but to love it and do it right (or at least perform the role of happy, perfect mom to continue the scam of Motherhood), raging at our families feels like the ultimate taboo. It is the opposite of what we were taught mothers are supposed to be like. Raging is not gentle, not kind, not nurturing, not affectionate, and not supportive.

In essence, raging is anti-Mother. But raging is *not* anti-father.

In Western culture, fathers get to be anything they want. They can be kind or domineering (or both!) because fathers aren't wholly defined by their fatherhood. It is not considered their highest calling. Fatherhood is a side gig. Dads are not in the midst of the greatest identity battle of their lives, disoriented and flailing as they become new selves. Fathers get to stay who they are when they have kids, whereas moms are just Mother.

So, if raging is anti-Mother, and Mother is all we are, then all we are is bad.

Under the patriarchal institution of motherhood, all the visible and invisible labor mothers do (picking the kids up from school, meal planning, researching summer camps, scheduling the dad's next colonoscopy) is in service to the interests of men. Each one is a tiny gift of freedom the mother grants the father. Because she has done the labor, he doesn't have to. While fathers may have their own laundry lists of personal gripes, their entire lives have not been usurped to serve the interests of women.

If dads could take in these nuances, and understand that mom rage is an experience rooted in misogyny and the disempowering gender dynamics of patriarchy, they would see that mom rage is much more complicated than moms getting "too mad." And, hopefully, this understanding can expand dads' compassion for the mothers they love, minimizing the distance between them. A father who gets it might even reach for the mother's spinning body, pull her from the shame spiral, and rock her gently, his body a safe mother place.

I am always learning about mom rage. I teach Paul as I go. This is emotional labor, but I need him to be with me. To understand me. I can't say Paul never disappears to his enemy island. Sometimes he vacations there. But it always helps to treat Paul as an ally, to ask him to show me what I cannot see, and in return to show him what he is missing. Paul and I are good at this sort of mutuality.

When I leaned against Paul on a rock in a Pacific Northwest river the summer I was twenty-six, I blurted out, "D'you wanna marry me?" He nodded, teary, then proposed in return, "Do you wanna marry *me*?" He has always tried to meet me where I am. Even when I make it hard. When I rescued Paul from enemy territory by asking him to look for my physical rage tells, I was inviting him to rescue me back. And he did. It was a mutual rescue, our favorite kind.

8 BETTER POLICY? YES, AND . . .

Women all over the United States must rally together to demand that tax money spent on the
arms race and other militaristic goals be spent on
improving the quality of parenting and child care
in this society.

—bell hooks, *Feminist Theory: From Margin to Center*

Mom rage has many arms, so to soothe it we have to hold
all its hands. So far, we've learned about the valuable and
necessary introspective work that helps alleviate mom rage. We've
understood how our anger fits into the Mom Rage Cycle. We've
learned how to increase our awareness of our patterns and triggers
by inviting our rage to tea. And we've considered how we might
enlist our partners as allies. This work, combined with therapy
and reading, writing, and thinking about mom rage, has been a
lifeline for me and many of the moms I interviewed. Now I'm
going to zoom out and focus on the society-wide solutions and
cultural shifts required to truly end mom rage. Because as long as

the mom-rage-inducing cultural architecture remains the same, we're never going to stop being mad.

We can breathe in one nostril and out the other all day, but when the baby wakes up again and again in the middle of the night, will that breathwork make the father wrest himself from sleep, then willingly show up at work with red-rimmed eyes so that the mother can be well-rested for her nonstop day of care work? We can rise before dawn, legs crossed, eyes closed, and meditate till the sun pierces the sky, but all the *om shantis* in the world won't strong-arm our country into giving us paid family leave.

If we return to the metaphor of mom rage as a multistory house, we can think of the self-work as alleviating those furious outbursts in the kitchen. The self-work slows us down so we can see the two paths that lie in front of us. One leads to an uncontrolled firestorm of anger, and the other to a more compassionate response. The self-work increases our capability to stop and think before we react.

Even if we master the art of empathy and manage to quiet the yells in our bellies, the rage will fester until we fully renovate the basement. I'm talking about doing away with the PR team and its messaging that indoctrinates us into thinking that a mother is inherently better at care work, and that a stay-at-home dad is a man who has failed to launch. I'm talking about seeing the care work of parenting as actual work that benefits society, and compensating it as such. I'm talking about a complete overhaul of the healthcare system that results in comprehensive, long-term maternal care. And I'm talking about the dissolution of gender, patriarchy, capitalism, and white supremacy. That is what really needs to happen to take the rage out of modern motherhood.

But let's begin with something more concrete: policy. Better policy won't eradicate mom rage without broader culture change. The good news is that as much as culture influences policy, policy can also influence culture. Think of the millions of mothers who would get a monthly reprieve of thousands of dollars if preschool were free and guaranteed for every child. Imagine what moms who can't afford the cost of preschool could do with forty to fifty extra hours a week. They could work. They could create. They could take care of themselves.

In the US, where mothercare policy is flagrantly absent or in-consequential, getting the right policies put in place can alleviate mom rage, improve the culture of motherhood, and save mothers' lives.

Above all else, birthing people must be able to choose when, if at all, they want to have children. We need accessible, free, and legal access to all birth control, including abortion, and free access to fertility interventions like IVF. We need policy that ensures all birthing people are provided with free, culturally competent pre-natal and birthing care. Everyone should have the free option of a midwife and doula dedicated to supporting them for pregnancy, birth, and postpartum care.

The postpartum period needs to be expanded in the culture's mind and medical definitions to a full year after birth, so mothers receive culturally competent services and support for that length of time. This support should include medical and mental health services, including lactation support, a night doula, and pelvic floor therapy. All practitioners should be available for home visits to accommodate mothers who have access barriers.

With the expansion of care in the postpartum period, all par-ents need the option of fully paid parental leave for a year, regard-less of biological relation to the child or marital status. That leave must be flexible so partners can divvy it up however best suits their family. To counteract toxic workplace culture that discour-ages fathers from taking their parental leave, incentives need to be implemented so all parents take their full length of leave.

To replace our current "Money or Mommy" care system in the US, we need to implement care infrastructure that provides free or highly subsidized daycare, preschool, summer care, and after-school care that is high-quality, comprehensive, and culturally competent, for every child. Everyone doing care work, including all domestic workers, teachers, childcare staff, and eldercare workers, need to be paid a competitive wage with benefits.

And finally, there's the issue of money *for* Mommy. By eliminating the gender wage gap, the motherhood penalty, the fatherhood bonus, and racially based pay imbalances, policy has the power to elevate mothers' earning potential, freeing us from being financially dependent on a spouse. Additionally, all caregivers need a stipend that reflects the value of our necessary labor. For those who do full-time care work for a child or any family member who needs around-the-clock care, the wage should be commensurate to someone doing care work in the paid sector.

No country has implemented all these mothercare policies. But access to even some of these structural supports can directly ameliorate mom rage. Nora, a white working-class artist and jeweler in the Netherlands, lives in an apartment with her four-year-old daughter. The father is out of the picture, so Nora has been with her daughter all day every day for four years. Nora described her mom rage as "feminist rage." She said what she's actually angry about is that there isn't anyone to help her. "But there's only one person here who I can have a conflict with, and that's my child." Nora finally got a labor reprieve and some time to herself when her daughter turned four and was able to attend a state-funded year of preschool. As a result, Nora's mom rage dissipated.

Policy alone isn't enough; we also have to consider how the policy is enacted. Some countries have policies that give mothers free lactation support, a year and a half of paid leave, midwives who come to the home for weeks postpartum, and the right to return to your job after taking a family leave of three years. For American mothers, these policies sound like a dream. But the paper version of policy does not always match the reality.

After the birth of her daughter, in true-to-the-rumors Dutch form, a maternity nurse called a *kraamzorg* came to Nora's house every day for a week, monitoring how much milk the baby got and how often the baby peed and pooped. The *kraamzorg* also cleaned up around the house and washed the dishes. It is even in the *kraamzorg's* scope of duties to grocery shop for the mother.

As Nora described the *kraamzorg* to me, she could sense my awe even through my silence. "Compared to the US, it's probably paradise," she laughed. Before I could become too enamored, Nora cautioned me that the care felt clinical and was focused mostly on the baby. "I remember feeling like some kind of discarded baby husk," Nora said. "The Netherlands invests heavily in having structures in place. But they don't actually do their job in a social or empathetic way. The theory of it is amazing, but the execution leaves a lot to be desired."

Care policy doesn't necessarily translate to cared-for people. Policy comes up lacking unless it is created and implemented using an "ethic of care," a term coined by psychologist and ethicist Carol Gilligan in her 1982 book *In a Different Voice*. Gilligan says an ethic of care is grounded in relationships and "in the importance of everyone having a voice, being listened to carefully . . . and heard with respect." Instead of the current patriarchal American healthcare system that uses rules and regulations as its "impartial" guide, an ethic of care is a matriarchal model that focuses on the needs and desires of the individual. Care policy delivered within this framework would have personalization and connection at its heart.

With an ethic of care in mind, I want to return to Ceci's story. She is the mom who gave birth in San Francisco and had no *cuarentena* because she had no family to take care of her. She was given the postpartum mood disorder (PMAD) screening form and the results showed she was at risk. After an initial therapy intake, Ceci never returned. If we look at this story from an institutional standpoint, the system did its job: the questionnaire was administered; it identified a new mother at risk for a PMAD; she was given the information that she could use to get help.

The problem is, the policy doesn't have any room for the realities of the people it is meant to serve. Getting to the appointment with her newborn in tow was too much for Ceci. She had no family in the area to help with the baby, and her husband only took one week off work. The PMAD policy doesn't take into account that so many American mothers have no help: one in five children lives with a single mother, dads rarely take more than two weeks of leave, 63 percent of queer people live in states that won't give employees family leave if they have no biological or legal relationship to the child, and only 38 percent of Black and 28 percent of Latinx workers who are eligible for FMLA (the federal Family and Medical Leave Act) can actually use it without falling below 200 percent of the poverty line. The list goes on. Maternal health is full of policies like FMLA and the PMAD screener that are well-intentioned but inaccessible to the people who need them most.

Political scientist Joan Tronto believes that attending to people using an ethic of care requires us to pay attention not only to how care is given, but to how it is received. She insists that care has not transpired without a thorough evaluation of its effectiveness. A provider is not absolved of their care duty by simply telling the mother that she's at risk for postpartum anxiety and giving her a number to call. When operating from an ethic of care, medical providers and medical policy makers would need to evaluate if the care was properly administered. They'd be required to follow up to see if the patient accessed the care being offered. If they did, another follow-up would be required down the road to see if the patient's health improved. If it didn't, there needs to be an inquiry into the barriers that stood in the way, and how those barriers can be accounted for moving forward so the policy's intended care reaches the patient.

When we use an ethic of care, situational specifics aren't unnecessary details—they're guiding principles. If Ceci was treated with an ethic of care, the therapist she saw one time would have contacted Ceci to find out why she didn't return. Ceci would have told her that she had no one to leave the baby with, and it was just too challenging to schlep the baby around by herself. If the policy were created with an ethic of care, it would be in the scope of the therapist's job to make patient-centered allowances, like letting Ceci do video therapy or holding the sessions at Ceci's home.

I can hear the dissenting voices in my ear: *This model would cost more. Everything would take longer.* That may be true. But it's also true that patriarchal capitalism's emphasis on saving time and money has come at a tremendous cost to mothers. A matriarchal system based on an ethic of care would prioritize the comprehensive wellness of people over money and efficiency. In her book *Essential Labor: Mothering as Social Change*, Angela Garbes writes, "The work [of love and care] may seem inefficient, but love doesn't play by the same rules as the economy. The economy could stand to bend to the will of decency and care."

Care is more likely to be delivered with decency and a personalized touch when the caregivers feel connected to the people they are helping. When a program is intended to impact a certain community, the people who belong to that community should be the program's leaders and direct service providers. Why aren't we using this tried-and-true best practice when it comes to maternal health and mothercare policy? In the rooms where policy, medical education curricula, and training are created and implemented, we need Black, Indigenous, Asian, and Latinx moms. We need moms who are intimately familiar with poverty. We need teen moms, people who became moms in their late forties and early fifties, adoptive moms, foster moms, IVF moms, and moms who've had abortions, miscarriages, and stillbirths. We need moms with larger bodies, moms who were victims of obstetric abuse, moms living with mental illness, and moms with physical disabilities. We need immigrant moms running boardrooms and queer parents heading up birthing wards. A healthcare system for moms that is created, managed, and implemented by anyone other than a diverse group of moms compromises the health of all moms and birthing people.

Here is an example of a mothercare policy created by moms for moms. In Germany there are eighty government-funded health retreats called the *Kur*. (*Kur* literally translates to "cure.") The three-week retreats are for moms and sometimes their children (and a small percentage of dads) to recharge and improve their immune systems through hydrotherapy, fresh air, nutrition programs, and physical therapy. The *Kur* was started in the 1950s by Elly Heuss-Knapp, an activist, writer, and wife of West Germany's first president, and the program remains under the patronage of the wives of the German presidents today (nine of the twelve first ladies have themselves been mothers).

The *Kur* demonstrates how useful it can be to have mothers with a diversity of experiences at the helm of maternal health policy. Heuss-Knapp's own mother became mentally ill and left the family when Heuss-Knapp was only three years old, an experience that surely influenced the creation of these maternal wellness retreats. And as a mother herself, Heuss-Knapp would have known that "family vacation" is a misnomer. That's why, in the original iteration of the *Kur*, mothers attended without their children. (In the 1970s, the vision shifted to include kids, and childcare is provided for up to six hours a day.)

Despite being a policy that is by moms for moms, the resources don't meet the demand. Every year, only 47,000 mothers—who must qualify as having a strong need—get to attend a *Kur*. I would argue that all mothers, sick or healthy, rich or poor, have a strong need for a wellness vacation. But even if the *Kur* served only single mothers (of which there are 2.1 million in Germany), it would take over forty-four years to get every one of them to a *Kur*.

We already know that policy alone will not tear down the patriarchy. But policy can impact deeply embedded patriarchal norms that lead to mom rage. *Kur* policy could require the children's *other* parent—or a trustworthy family member if the other parent is ill, dead, unsafe, or nonexistent—to take care of the children during the mother's three-week *Kur*. German companies are already required to continue paying their employees during their *Kur*. If *Kur* policy required companies to also pay spouses so they could do full-time childcare, it could have long-term effects on the mental wellness of mothers and the culture of parenting in Germany.

Studies have shown that fathers who take parental leave are more involved in their children's lives for years to come, and have a more equal labor split in the home. Their marriages are significantly less likely to end in divorce. Mandated paid family leave for non-gestational parents is a direct line to mom rage alleviation.

In a study for the National Bureau of Economic Research, Stanford University economists looked at the effects of a Swedish policy that lets fathers use thirty days of their parental leave asynchronously, meaning they can take a day here, a day there, giving families—mothers in particular—help on the days they *actually* need it. The results were a 26 percent decrease in moms' antianxiety prescriptions, a 14 percent decrease in moms' visits to specialists and hospitalizations, and an 11 percent decrease in moms' antibiotic prescriptions, all in the first six months postpartum.

Pro-mother policies that actually reach mothers have long-term health benefits. Another study documented that a long maternity leave decreased mothers' depression by 18 percent even thirty years later. Mauricio Avendano, one of the authors of that study, says these kinds of policies are "what economists call a human capital investment. You invest in this, you will end up picking up the benefits of this policy even years later." Despite an initial increase in cost and time, front-loading preventative care for parents—whether it's a year's worth of video therapy or a requirement for employees to take the entire length of their fully paid parental leave—saves the state time and money years down the line, and helps make the home environment more equitable and less filled with rage.

The mothercare policies I've outlined are not a pipedream. Some of them have been signed into law before. Access to safe and legal abortion was a federally upheld right for nearly fifty years until it was struck down in 2022. We also have a blueprint for the implementation of universal daycare and preschool from the last time the federal government set up this structural piece of mothercare—in the 1940s.

Through what's commonly known as the Lanham Act, the US government spent $52 million (which would be close to one billion dollars today) from 1943 to 1946 to subsidize childcare across the country so more mothers could take jobs in factories to keep the war effort humming until the soldiers returned. At its peak, there were 3,102 federally subsidized nurseries and care centers. Childcare was offered six days a week, including summers and holidays. The centers had low student-to-teacher ratios and served meals and snacks. Parents paid a small daily fee, the equivalent of nine or ten dollars today.

How did mothers win this comprehensive, affordable, quality childcare infrastructure? It was not due to a sweeping cultural attitude adjustment. Public sentiment at the time was that mothers should be with their children. Mayor La Guardia said in 1943, "The worst mother is better than the best institution when it is a matter of child care." It is doubtful the 535 members of the seventy-sixth United States Congress (nine were women) implemented these nurseries so mothers could have fully realized lives that didn't revolve completely around care work.

Mothers got federally funded childcare because lawmakers believed the need for production was great enough that it superseded their own moralistic values on motherhood. The Lanham Act was not an acknowledgment of the value of mothers' domestic labor. It merely acknowledged that women's labor outside the home was desperately needed—temporarily. When the men returned from war, the nurseries and the money that funded them disappeared.

If we fast forward eighty years to 2021, we find an example of another major mothercare policy being passed during a worldwide emergency. For six months, American families received a stipend of up to three hundred dollars per child each month under President Biden's American Rescue Plan, which aimed to ameliorate some of the financial hardships families were facing during the pandemic. The expanded Child Tax Credit is reminiscent of the Lanham Act in that it was an emergency measure. But it is monumental in that it was a trial run of paying parents a monthly child allowance. In its first month, three million children were lifted out of poverty. Since we know from Ou and Hall's research that economic hardship is one of the three factors that lead to mothers feeling powerless and angry, the expanded Child Tax Credit is another policy solution for alleviating mom rage.

The monthly stipends dried up when the original version of Biden's Build Back Better bill didn't get the support it needed in the Senate. In addition to continuing the expanded Child Tax Credit, Build Back Better would have implemented paid family leave and universal preschool for all three- and four-year-olds, halved the price of childcare for most families, and provided the elderly and people with disabilities with higher quality care in their homes while also offering higher pay for professionals doing the care work. The original bill was acknowledging and paying for care work, treating it as necessary societal infrastructure—and it almost passed! We are getting closer to gaining the mothercare policies we need.

Even when a policy doesn't pass or is discontinued, its brief existence is still a win for shifting the mothercare conversation forward. Every policy sets a precedent for more policies like it in the future. The expanded Child Tax Credit is the great-grandchild of a long line of efforts to pay women and mothers for childcare and domestic labor.

The International Feminist Collective was an activist Marxist group that launched the Wages for Housework (WFH) campaign in 1972. It argued that women should receive a wage for motherhood, which they called "reproductive labor." Reproductive labor is the work needed to create and sustain the next generation, including growing and birthing babies, childcare, cleaning, household management, and emotional labor. WFH posited that the societal expectation for women to birth and care for humanity—work that is the lynchpin for productivity and profit—is exploitation. They positioned WFH as a class struggle by identifying reproductive labor as "unwaged," and the people doing that labor as "wageless workers."

WFH was inspired in part by another powerful effort to pay mothers. In the 1960s the National Welfare Rights Organization

(NWRO) was led by Johnnie Tillmon, mother of six. The movement had 25,000 members at its height, mostly poor Black mothers, despite welfare recipients being majority white. NWRO fought for an adequate income for mothers, regardless of whether they did paid work outside the home or unpaid work inside the home. This was an important and distinct voice from the mostly white middle-class women's movement that was calling for the right to work outside of the home.

The work of the various factions of the women's movement in the US during the 1960s and 1970s, including NWRO and WFH, inspired the birth of women's movements around the world. One of them was the Redstockings in Iceland. Their focus was directed at closing the gender wage gap, demanding equal labor in the home, creating daycare centers, and securing women's right to abortion.

The Redstockings figured out how to make the country's fathers see the value of women's labor. On October 24, 1975, 90 percent of the women in Iceland, in every part of the country, participated in a labor strike called Women's Day Off. The day was in protest of Iceland's gender-based wage discrimination. At that time, an Icelandic company would explicitly say they were looking to fill a position with a woman. This was because women's salaries were so much lower than men's. On the day of the strike, women didn't go to offices, cook, clean, or take care of children. Schools shut down. The national airline canceled flights. Men were forced to bring their children to work. Kids could be heard in the background of news reports on the radio.

The strike changed the society. The following year, Iceland passed a law that banned gender-based wage discrimination. Five years later, Vigdís Finnbogadóttir, a divorced single mother, became the first woman in the world to be democratically elected as a head of state. She stayed in that position for sixteen years.

Remembering Women's Day Off, she said to the BBC, "So many companies and institutions came to a halt, and it showed the force and necessity of women—it completely changed the way of thinking." When the strike happened, there were only three women members of Iceland's parliament. Now they make up 44 percent. In 2000, the country implemented paid family leave for both parents. Eighty-two percent of fathers in Iceland take their leave.

The work to support caregivers through policy has been happening for a long time, and every bit of it helps turn the rusty wheel of change. Still, there is so much more to do. Mothers need help. The activism to structurally, emotionally, and financially support all who do care work cannot rest solely on the shoulders of exhausted mothers and overworked, underpaid domestic workers and caregivers. We need allies without kids. And we need fathers to use their privilege in the streets, boardrooms, and the halls of Congress to fight for universal childcare, paid family leave, safe and competent pregnancy and postpartum care, the right to have autonomy over our own bodies, equal pay for equal work, and a fair wage for all care workers inside and outside of the home. We need dads to get angry! *And* make dinner! Everyone should be raging!

Collectively agitating for policy reform to support caregivers and reduce mom rage is necessary work that never ends (at least not in my lifetime). But we can't give up. Despite huge victories for the women of Iceland in 1975, their gender wage gap has not completely disappeared, so the unified effort of Iceland's women continues. In 2005, they walked out of work at 2:08 p.m., the time of day when their pay stops if they were making what men make. In 2008, they walked out at 2:25. In 2016, it was 2:38. Equality is a slow and persistent labor.

While we continue organizing to create and pass policies that will give us the federally funded care infrastructure we need, mothers must take care of ourselves by continuing to weave our own care safety nets and accessing the most powerful resource of all—each other.

9   BEYOND THE NUCLEAR FAMILY

> Do you understand that your quality of life and
> your survival are tied to how authentic and gener-
> ous the connections are between you and the peo-
> ple and place you live with and in?
>
> —adrienne maree brown, *Emergent Strategy:*
> *Shaping Change, Changing Worlds*

Until we have the policies and infrastructure mothers need to take care of our families and ourselves, every single mom is left to find individual solutions for our collective abandonment. Mothers never felt more abandoned by society than during the COVID-19 pandemic. With schools closed and the kids home all day, the pressure, workload, and isolation ratcheted up our rage until it was an electric current in the air we were trying not to breathe. To ease the strain on families and specifically mothers, many people formed pandemic "pods," small groups of people, like two families, who abided by agreed-upon COVID precautions and essentially shared air by being inside each other's homes. Some pods shared everything from dinner to childcare. It was a

COVID-forced, micro-version of community, and in some cases, collective mothering.

After five months of it being just Mae, Ollie, Paul, and me, with no childcare or community whatsoever, my family formed a pod with my in-laws, Moshe and Shlomit. When Ollie stayed home to do second grade online, Mae went to play at her grandparents' house three times a week.

Moshe is no slouch, but Shlomit is the childcare hero of this story. I'd pick Mae up and often find the two of them pretending to be cats on the floor under a blanket, licking their "paws." Shlomit has a knack for seeing exactly who people are and what they need. She does it with me, too, inviting me to lunch, intuiting that I am stretched for time but desperately want to be taken care of. Mothered. "You gotta eat, right?" she says persuasively.

We were lucky and grateful to have this help. Being podded with my in-laws meant we could spend time at their house, only twenty minutes away. After months of memorizing every crack and dirt streak decorating the walls of our own home, it was a relief to be in their clean, multistory house, filled with orchids, sunlight, and the smell of delicious food I didn't have to cook. Shlomit and Moshe provided fresh juice, laughter, a break. They'd talk to Paul and me about grown-up things and indulge the kids in their child interests, which Paul and I were often too weary to do. They were the pressure release valve of community that my family desperately needed. I'm pretty sure the feeling was mutual.

The impossibility of being home with the kids while working full time presented families with an opportunity to do things differently during that first year of the pandemic. For many, there was really no other choice. Nuclear families who had already been struggling prepandemic ground to halt. The benefits of intentional community and alternative family structures became clear, even to white middle-class families, who are least likely to live in multigenerational households. All it took was a worldwide pandemic.

Despite the throne the nuclear family sits on in America's collective consciousness, its heyday was a brief fifteen-year period from 1950 to 1965, when 73 percent of American children lived in a household with two married parents in their first marriage. (By 2015 that number had dropped to 46 percent.) After the men returned from fighting in World War II, and the factories where the mothers had worked in their absence closed along with the federally funded childcare centers, Motherhood's PR team had to convince mothers to go back to their housewife lives. "This was orchestrated and facilitated by an ideological redesign of what constitutes good motherhood," writes founder of Demeter Press Andrea O'Reilly. "Two beliefs emerged in the 1950s: 1) children require full time 'stay-at-home' mothering; and 2) children, without full time mothering, would suffer from what was termed 'maternal deprivation.'"

The cult of the nuclear family commanded so much power during its peak that in a 1957 survey from the University of Michigan, 80 percent of those surveyed thought that people who chose not to marry were sick, immoral, or neurotic. When we center one way of being as normal, all other ways get denigrated to abnormal or "less good."

Framing the nuclear family as a moral requirement creates the kind of pressure that's needed to convince an entire nation to isolate their families within a structure that is inherently unstable. Balancing a family's well-being on only two support beams (the parents) leaves no room for parental needs, let alone inevitable mishaps. No matter how streamlined the parents have set their lives up to be—well-paying jobs with health insurance, kids in childcare, grocery shopping every Tuesday, church every Sunday—something will blow their house down. A family member will fall ill. A parent will lose their job. Parents will get divorced and one will move far away. Someone will struggle with addiction. When these unforeseen circumstances happen, the entire family is left to balance on one parent—a lone teetering support beam. Even without a major event causing havoc, the isolated nuclear family is a structure in danger of collapse.

Being underresourced in an insular family structure and by society steers us toward parental burnout, which is how 66 percent of parents described feeling in a 2022 poll. In her *New York Times* article, "How Society Has Turned Its Back on Mothers," Pooja Lakshmin, a psychiatrist specializing in women's health, argues that the term *burnout* blames the individual (often the mom) for not being resilient enough, whereas "betrayal . . . points directly to the broken structures around them." Society's betrayal of mothers makes us exhausted, overwhelmed, and overworked, which all lead to short fuses, which lead to mom rage.

The structure of the nuclear family then sequesters raging mothers behind the walls of our individual homes, with no other mothers or family to take some of the burden. In *How We Show Up: Reclaiming Family, Friendship, and Community*, Mia Birdsong writes that the nuclear family is an example of "toxic individualism": rather than building a structure of communal support to lift all families, each family struggles to get the resources it needs, cordoned off in its own little home, creating a perfectly caulked box for fury.

In the US, the nuclear family is touted as the only family model (and fiscally rewarded accordingly), as if other structures have not always existed and don't continue to do so. In many parts of the world, children were and are still taken care of by many people— blood-related and not. Anthropologist Sarah Blaffer Hrdy showed this in her work with the Efé people in what is now the Democratic Republic of the Congo. By time infants are six weeks old, they are mostly cared for by people who are *not* their birth mother. Margaret Mead talked about older siblings (as young as six years old) in Samoa being the primary carers for their baby and toddler siblings.

The need for more capable hands may be why multigenerational households have quadrupled in the US since 1971. The top two reasons people list for this way of living? Finances and caregiving. A quarter of Black, Asian, and Hispanic families in the US live in multigenerational households, along with 13 percent of white families.

Alternative family structures are born of necessity or ideology, or sometimes a mix of the two. Black families in America have long utilized extended family and community to help with child-rearing, a practice rooted in West African culture but made essential during slavery, when families were routinely ripped apart. The flexibility of Black families makes room for *othermothers*, who sociologist Patricia Hill Collins describes as "women who assist blood mothers by sharing mothering responsibilities." An othermother might be a community elder, cousin, or auntie who isn't actually related. Othermothers contribute to a culture of Black motherhood that writer Ashley Simpo describes as "expansive and cooperative."

Queer people have also broadened family beyond biology. One queer family I know has two gay dads and two gay moms. They co-parent their son in their separate homes, like a typical fifty-fifty custody arrangement but without the divorce. Even for queer people who are living in more typical nuclear families, many have "found families" or "chosen families"—people they've deliberately selected for family-like care and support. The wider spectrum of possibility for some Black and queer families is both an act of survival under the destructive forces of structural racism and homophobia, and a creative strength that casts parenting responsibilities across a larger net of care.

There are numerous ways to create non-nuclear family structures that offer mothers more support. After her divorce, Frannie,
the bisexual Taiwanese Canadian mom of two tweens, stum-
bled into her own alternative family support structure through
a dating app. As she swiped through potential partners, she was
surprised to see that many people listed themselves as "ethically
non-monogamous." *What is this?* Frannie wondered. She soon
found out that ethical or consensual non-monogamy (ENM/
CNM) is an umbrella term for people who are intimate, sexually
and/or romantically, with more than one partner with everyone's
consent. Polyamory—a well-known form of ENM—is the relationship orientation of being open to having multiple intimate
(romantic and/or sexual) relationships at the same time. Recent
studies put the American ENM population between 4 and 10
percent.

Frannie began dating Gerald, a polyamorous married man,
who lives with his wife, Alisha. Alisha also has her own boyfriend. Though Frannie was romantically involved only with
Gerald, who soon became her boyfriend, all of them—Frannie,
Gerald, Alisha, and Alisha's boyfriend, along with Frannie's
kids—became an alternative family unit. They spent holidays like
Thanksgiving together. When Frannie's daughter had trouble in
math, Frannie didn't have to spend her evening hours searching
for a tutor or scrounging up funds to pay for one. Gerald's wife,
Alisha, is a mathematician, and she volunteered to do it: "Alisha
made math fun for my daughter. I was really touched by that."

Frannie remembered Gerald and Alisha asking how they
could ease some of her burdens: "Just having them ask, 'What
can I do to support you?' was huge! My ex-husband would have
never asked that." Frannie told them, and from then on Gerald
drove Frannie's daughter to her rock-climbing class. The four
adults shared a love of cooking, which resulted in direct relief for

Frannie. Whether it was takeout or an elaborate meal, the four of them were often messaging each other to come on over and eat.

Chauffeuring kids to extracurricular activities and making a family's meals is so much time and effort, especially for moms like Frannie who are in school and working paid jobs. But in this alternative structure, with four able and willing adults, "it wasn't all on one person. The labor was shared. Just having the daily tasks made easier was amazing." Not to mention the financial benefits: the four of them would split costs for special holiday meals, making them more affordable for everyone, and Gerald contributed a quarter of Frannie's rent, since he was at her house so often.

Frannie and Gerald are no longer together, and she's not sure whether her next relationship will be non-monogamous. But Frannie says that's not really what's important for staving off overwhelm and rage. What matters is the pooling of resources and the support that expanded family structures can offer: "We can have intimacy with platonic friends and still share labor."

Without the nourishment and necessary support of an alternative family structure like Frannie's, many parents turn to members of their own nuclear families, especially to their own parents. Almost a third of children of mothers who work paid jobs are cared for by grandparents. But relying on grandparents for childcare comes with its own set of complications.

I count my family as one of my biggest privileges in life. I hit the jackpot, both with my birth family and the one I married into. I see or talk to someone in my extended family almost every day, and I know, perhaps more than anything else in life, that I am deeply loved by them. Paul and I live a thirty-minute drive from countless family members. And we still cannot get a break from parenting.

Paul and I take good care of each other. He solo parents while I go to a weeklong writing residency. I solo parent while he visits a friend in another state. This is the way we have figured out how to take time for ourselves. But we cannot seem to take time away as a couple. Once, we managed to steal away for two consecutive nights for our ten-year anniversary. To make that happen, his parents took the kids for one night, and my parents flew across the country from Philadelphia to stay at our house and care for the kids for the other night. That was four years ago.

A year into the pandemic, fresh vaccines in our arms, Paul and I fantasized about going on a vacation together, just the two of us, far, far away. *The kids are older now*, we thought. Maybe his parents could take three nights and my parents could fly out again and take three nights. I imagined my feet sinking into the warm, white sand, turquoise water lapping at the shore. I pictured us in reclining beach chairs, drinks with colorful umbrellas in our hands. I could almost feel the sun on my legs. But the answer was no.

Sometimes I wonder if both sets of grandparents don't want to take our kids for multiple nights because we have high-energy children. Ollie knows just how to push Mae's buttons. Mae knows just how to whine and cry in that perfect pitch that presses grown-ups' buttons. It feels impossible not to get involved, not to get annoyed. *Ollie, be kind! Mae, stop whining!* I understand that parenting them, while delightful and snuggly and rewarding, is challenging, especially for four septuagenarians. Is any child truly compliant, though? I suspect the grandparents are just tired. *I'm* tired, and I'm half their age.

For those of us who've moved far away from our families of origin, we are lucky if our parents are well enough and have the financial means to visit their grandchildren. But if they do, both parents and grandparents are often under the false pretense their visit will be helpful.

Elizabeth, the community college English professor who lives in Seattle with her carpenter wife and two children, needs help during parent-teacher conference week, when her kids will have half days at school. Her mother volunteers to fly across the country, which will make it possible for Elizabeth to work full days at her job that week.

Despite best intentions, grandparent visits are often more taxing than useful. In the weeks leading up to her trip, Elizabeth's mom calls and says things, like, "Well, you know, I'm wondering what you want me to do with them," and "I like to take a nap at one o'clock. Are you going to be home for part of that?" Elizabeth tells me, "At the end of the day, it's like, now I have this extra person to take care of during conference week. This actually hasn't lightened my load at all."

Elizabeth fantasizes about having another adult to help out. "By nature, I'm very monogamous, so I don't fantasize about it in any sense other than wanting the relief of having a third person. My fantasy is not having someone who I can pay, but somebody who's fluidly woven into the fabric of our family, who could just step in without it being a big effort." That person, however, is not Elizabeth's mother.

Because of the grind of capitalism—working to save enough to be able to retire at age sixty-five—who wants to then devote themselves to taking care of children in the last active decades of their lives? I hate that I asked my seventy-five-year-old mom to get on a plane and take care of my kids. And when she told me no, I hate that I slid into despair. *There is no one to help us!* The nuclear family structure is one of scarcity. It leans so heavily on mothers to do the childcare, that when mothers can't do it, and their mothers also can't do it, that's the end of the line. I feel defensive of grandmothers. Haven't they earned the right to stop doing care work? Why do mothers-turned-grandmothers have to caregive until they die? *Please let us rest!*

I dream of living in a community with other families and sharing land but having our own home, with an open-door feel. I want group dinners, too many emergency contacts to choose from, and all the kids in the community to feel like ours. Paul and I tried to make this happen once but were priced out of the market and haven't figured out how to make our cohousing fantasy a reality in the Bay Area, especially while we're busy running the rat race of raising children in a nuclear family during late-stage capitalism. To break free of the nuclear family's toxic individualism, and to alleviate the mom rage it stokes, I have begun to forge community in small ways. I do this mostly through an informal exchange of favors—a ride here, a container of meatballs there.

In *The Art of Asking*, musician Amanda Palmer writes that if you want to make someone your friend, ask them for a favor. I've discovered that a favor is also a good place to begin if you want to expand your care network.

My cousin Julia and her husband, Jonah, live two miles from us. I love them and their two daughters. The littlest is only two and I barely know her because she was born just before the pandemic began. I decided I needed to take the expansion of our care network into my own hands.

"Give us your children," read the subject heading of the email I wrote Julia and Jonah. I pressed *Send* with a proud click. I'd never felt resourced enough to be able to take care of more children than my own. But with Ollie and Mae getting more manageable, and both of them now attending school in person, things have eased up some. Or maybe I'm finally settling into motherhood. Sometimes it takes a decade, right?

Jonah called me to discuss cousin playdate logistics, and then asked for a favor—could Paul and I watch their kids overnight in a few months? My cousins were planning a five-day trip for their ten-year anniversary and were cobbling together a team of friends and family to care for their kids. "Of course," I said, touched that he had asked me. *Gosh*, I thought, *if my cousins are taking a five-day trip by asking favors from their community, why couldn't we?* Maybe I've been thinking about it all wrong. I don't have to wallow in vacationless self-pity just because the grand-parents aren't able to babysit for a week. I can lean on my community. By offering to care for my cousin's kids, I positioned my family deeper into their support network, and as a result, they have solidified into a stronger part of mine.

Though Paul and I do not have the cohousing life or the alter-native family structure I dream about, we have formed connections that help ease the strain and isolation of parenting in a nuclear family. We now exchange babysitting with Julia and Jonah and another friend who lives a few blocks away. This simple and crucial support network allows Paul and me to spend time together without children. When we get to be out in the world together, we are easier on each other back inside the walls of our home.

Our community built on favors includes our neighbors. When we moved into our bungalow home almost ten years ago, we lucked out to live next door to Herman and Carolyn. They are an elderly Black couple who've been in their house for fifty-seven years. I periodically bring them gifts in the form of food: sugar cookies from the kids' holiday cookie-cutting extravaganza, half a lasagna or leftover kugel. (I always seem to cook for an army.)

When Ollie turned one, Carolyn and Herman gifted him one of those pusher toys for toddlers learning to walk. They started leaving offerings on our doorstep, too: a paper bag with plums from their tree, a loaf of iced cinnamon bread that the kids go crazy for. Each gift is a surprise delight, a little relief from the everyday grind.

Over time, some of the gifts have become more important. Herman passed away in 2020. During the pandemic, Carolyn, newly widowed, had knee surgery. I stopped by to check on her and saw she had no ice packs. I ran home to grab mine, happy to have a clear way I could be of service. Soon after, Carolyn's daughter, who lives with her, offered me an appointment to get my first COVID vaccine shot at the health clinic where she works.

Maybe for some people, this is just being neighborly, but to me it's a multigenerational support network. Carolyn and her family are part of our community, built on the informal exchange of favors, which is just another way to say "care." These seemingly small favors are daily reprieves of a support network outside of the nuclear family.

The exchange of community care in all its forms is a necessary resource for moms, so that we are not always worn down to irritated threads. Stress, overwhelm, isolation, and relationship struggles can all bubble over into explosive rage if we don't get respite. Little things add up to big stress. And simple favors amount to big relief: a neighbor brings us fruit, and I can put off going to the store for one more day; another parent agrees to give Ollie a ride home from after-school care, then I can take the family car to my writing retreat; a babysitting swap provides me with space to reconnect to a self that is not only mother. These small acts of service are life preservers in a society that refuses to support mothers and families. Yet the toxic individualism of the nuclear family is so strong that asking for favors from outside the family can feel like a breach of loyalty or a motherhood failure. In actuality, they're motherhood victories that strengthen not only the stability of the family but the community as a whole.

I have also been nurturing community supports specifically for my rage. This is both preventative and restorative. Talking about my family life and parenting struggles helps take the air out of my anxiety and stress so they don't balloon into rage. Paul cannot—and should not be expected to—meet all of my emotional needs. As the other overtaxed support beam of our nuclear family, Paul is sometimes too overwhelmed himself to access the empathic wisdom and generosity I need. Also, Paul is not a mom. He's "gets" mom rage as well as a dad can, but I'm not sure he can ever *get* it in the way other mothers do.

Engaging with my mom rage community about my rage can shorten or eliminate my Shame Spiral phase. Professionals, like my therapist Nat, hold the bigger picture for me when I can only see the black dot of self-hatred. They remind me of all that I have going on and the unsupportive structures and systems I am up against.

As a white middle-class Jewish East Coaster, and daughter of a Brooklynite, being in therapy is practically my birthright. But therapy is not a good fit for everyone. Even sliding-scale therapy can be financially prohibitive, and it is still viewed as taboo in some communities. Luckily, mom friends are free and require no appointment. They help me to give myself what I can't seem to on my own—kindness, empathy, forgiveness. When I am feeling my most wretched, I need other mothers who intimately recognize the shape of my grief, mothers who can tell me their own stories to pull me out of the depths of mine.

Denise is one of my mom-rage go-to friends. She has two neurodivergent kids of her own. Sometimes we text each other after kid bedtime: *Walk?* On our stroll around the neighborhood, I confess I yelled at Ollie and I feel bad. I tell her I'd gotten a phone call from Ollie's counselor on day four of a new summer camp, and how I could feel every inch of my skin prickle as the counselor spoke and the story of Ollie's behavior unfolded. I recount what the counselor told me to Denise.

"Oh, good, so it's not just me," Denise responds, surprising me. I turn to her, my eyes wide.

"What happened with yours?" I ask, feeling myself lighten.

Denise tells me she got a phone call to inform her that her kindergartener has been walking around camp saying, "Fucking idiot!" I clap my hand over my mouth, and we both laugh, letting the bigness of our hard things deflate into humor. There's relief in being known and fully seen without having to explain myself. Community is anti-isolation.

Most of the mothers I interviewed said their go-to mom-rage support people are other mothers. One said, "I have a lot of judgment of myself, so having friends who say, 'I've yelled at my kids, I've done this thing too,' has been my lifeline." Finding people who intimately know the curve and tenor of your struggles is a self-loving practice rooted in community care. It takes us out of the screamscape of our minds, where anger and self-punishment rule with iron fists. And lands us in the arms of people who hold our wellness as a priority.

It is a transgressive act to maintain the vulnerability required to form relationships under systemic oppression. Mothers' vulnerability (which is enormous and ever-present, even if we safeguard it with yelling or by appearing to have it all together) and the relationships we form with others are strengths that sustain us. Picking up another mom's kids when they get sick at school and the parents can't get there in time; dropping off clothes your kids have outgrown to another mom; asking, offering, and accepting favors—these are not trite ways of saying "just be kind." They are community mothering. They are stepping up and taking care of other mothers and families, as mothers have always done when society won't.

With all the ways we are set up to shrink inside the buzzing taskwork of our mothering lives, mothers sometimes forget the great expanse of our capacity. This is when we call on our support network—the mom friends who truly get it, the othermothers, the chosen family, the babas, the moppas, the aunties, even the special fathers—the people who will sweep in and care for our kids, the ones who also plead for our help, reminding us that we can take care of them right back. These are the ones who rescue us, who respond to our post-rage shame texts with the right words:

You think that's bad? You should've been at my house tonight . . .

Ew, sounds like he was being a jerk.

I'm coming over with wine.

You'll hug them in the morning, and no one will even remember what you're saying sorry for.

The kids will be fine.

You are a good mom.

ACKNOWLEDGMENTS

This book is thanks to the labor and love of an array of mothers and our allies.

It is no small act of bravery to say to a stranger, "Yes, you can interview me about my deep and churning fury." Thanks to the mamas for trusting me and for contributing to the expansion of the dialogue on modern motherhood.

Nicole James knew the world needed this book well before I did. Thank you for the many hours we spent on the phone writing the proposal during that sinkhole first year of the pandemic, our children clawing at our closed office/bedroom doors as we forged ahead with the work. I am forever grateful to you for being my book partner and champion the whole way through.

Much appreciation to Charlotte Sheedy for getting my essay "The Rage Mothers Don't Talk About" into the hands of Jess Grose at the *New York Times*. Jess, if you had not believed mom rage was a topic deserving of amplification, none of this would have happened.

I was lucky enough to work with multiple powerhouse women at Seal Press. Emi Ikkanda, thank you for acquiring *Mom Rage* and for holding social change as the focus. Emma Berry, you whipped this book into shape from a drastically different first draft! Thank you for making me feel like all my parts were allowed in this book, and, along with Marissa Koors, for holding the larger picture when I was flailing among the sentences. Gratitude to the entire production, design, and marketing and publicity teams.

My writing voice has been encouraged and molded by many mentors, including Caryn Mirriam-Goldberg, Lise Weil, Ellie Epp, Gary Lemons, and Jane Lazarre. Dorothy Allison's and Toni Morrison's books taught me that beauty and change can come from writing about hard things. Anne Lamott, thank you for holding the light and leading the way.

I am indebted to Heart Rage, my queer literary home. Your generous feedback on my messy early drafts made this book so much better. Big love to Max Pearl, Amy Butcher, Alisa Barnes, Ilana Kramer, Zaedryn Rook, Noadiah Eckman, Jen Cross, and Joe Garrett. Cowriting dates with Tomas Moniz and Elaine Lin Hering rescued me from my house and all the domestic shoulds.

Thank you to Jen Cross for Writing the Flood, where the initial wisps of my writing on mom rage felt safe enough to emerge. And to Ellen LaPointe, for always being a compass on what is ethical and loving and good. Your friendship and the way you've both understood and cheered on my work has been invaluable.

Retreats and discussions on marriage, divorce, sex, motherhood, and patriarchy with Patti Maciesz, Amanda Montei, Kaitlin Solimine, and Cindy DiTiberio were such a gift as this book came to life. Thanks to Amanda and Patti for your close reading on my mom labor pages.

Thanks to Macy Chadwick for the gift of residencies at In Cahoots, where I wrote Chapter 4.

Gratitude to Stella Fiore for your stewardship of Cut+Paste, Lenka Clayton for Artist Residency in Motherhood, and the Binders—an endless resource for women and nonbinary writers.

Phone calls, voice notes, emails, frantic mom rage texts, neighborhood walks, group chats—I am fortified every day by my friends. Thank you for being the ones who get it. Special nod to Tali Ratzon, who birthed Chapter 3, when, after listening to me yammer on, she innocently asked, "Isn't the PTA voluntary?"

My Bay Area family held me through the writing of this book and beyond. From babysitting to feeding me to clinking glasses at family dinners for each draft I submitted, I could not have been luckier in the family lottery. Moshe and Shlomit—I am grateful for the ways you mother us all.

I had the good fortune of being born into a family of writers. They taught me that word formation is art, a worthy vocation, a form of activism, and a puzzle to be enjoyed. Alex, thank you for letting me slay you in this book. Everything is your fault. I love you. Dad, the image of your wet eyes and proud face has been a motivating factor my entire life and especially while working on this book. Mom—my first call, my safe place, my coconspirator— thank you for always being in my corner and showing me how to coexist as a mother and an artist.

To my two cupcakes who made me a mama and changed my life for the better, watching you grow and come into your fierce, hilarious, tender selves is such a joy. You inspire, delight, and teach me every day. I love you forever.

And to my big love: everything, everything, everything. Thank you for seeing me and holding my hand no matter what. For your ceaseless support and your staunch belief in my work in the world. For being my equal partner in all things. For your re- bellious spirit and the permission it gives us to create a life exactly how we want. It's quite a thing to be loved by you.

APPENDIX

How Partners Benefit Professionally from Mothers Being the Primary Parent

1. If partners have a magical fairy who gets the children ready in the mornings, makes the lunches, and gets the kids to school, then partners can make it to work on time, early even. Early bird gets the worm!

2. Because non-primary parents don't have a running tally of the family's to-do list, their minds are not splintering into fragmented, multitasking mayhem. As a result, they get to sit down in a chair while they eat lunch! Or read an article in its entirety in one go! Or connect with a coworker! Or recharge, so they can finish up the second half of the workday with enough energy to bring that go-getter attitude!

3. Because non-primary parents aren't usually listed in the Parent/Guardian #1 slot on every contact form for their child, they get fewer interruptions during the workday. As a result, partners are able to focus and be productive employees with strong follow-through!

4. When partners don't have to leave work early to take kids to various appointments or take the day off every time a kid gets sick, they can be more cued in to the daily goings-on

at work. Their constant presence shines when the company looks to give a raise or promotion to a dedicated employee!

5. With moms holding it all down, partners can attend the Friday happy hour, or go on the work trip to meet the bosses at the New York office. Their faces are seen and their voices get heard—they become a player in the company.

For Partners: 19 Steps To Alleviate Your Co-parent's Mom Rage

1. **Make dinner (and other meals) from the *real* start to the *real* finish.*** That means meal planning for the week ahead; writing down all needed ingredients on the grocery list; doing the grocery shopping; cleaning the kitchen in preparation for cooking (may include unloading the dishwasher or dish rack); cooking the meal; getting the kids to set the table and wash their hands for dinner; serving the meal; being the point person who gets out of your chair to retrieve the seventeen things the kids request from the kitchen; clearing the table or hounding the kids to clear it; and cleaning/scrubbing/rinsing/sweeping/wiping until all evidence of a meal cooked and eaten has disappeared. Let your cleanup mantra be *No item left behind!*

2. **Do the dishes.** Like making dinner, dishes seem like a no-brainer. But every time I ask mothers to tell me one thing their partner could do to alleviate their stress, multiple mothers shout, "Do the motherfucking dishes!" Also, use soap. On every dish.

---

* Inspired by Eve Rodsky's "Conceive. Plan. Execute. (CPE)" idea in *Fair Play: A Game-Changing Solution for When You Have Too Much to Do (and More Life to Live)*.

3. **Be on top of the kids' daily, weekly, and annual schedules, including school holidays.** Enter their schedules and school holidays on your personal and shared calendars. Look at your calendar daily. Look at the week and month ahead. Know when your kid has a test so you can make sure they're prepared. Know which day of the week is library day at school so you can remind them to put their library books in their backpacks. Initiate conversations with the mom you love about school holiday childcare options. Offer to do the childcare for some of them yourself. Or be in charge of getting childcare help, from the *real* start to the *real* finish: research and find a sitter with plenty of time so you don't end up in the I-found-one-but-they-fell-through situation; handle all communication and scheduling with the sitter; coordinate what food the sitter will give the kids and what sustenance the sitter themself will need; find and set out a spare key for the sitter; write down the phone numbers and any pertinent information the sitter might need; go to the bank to get cash; pay the sitter and make sure they have a safe way to get home.

4. **Be the point person on communication with other adults about your child.** Initiate contact and build positive relationships with adults who interact with your kid. Ask the mother you love to include you on any emails she writes involving your child, so she doesn't have the additional task of rehashing the communication she had with the teacher or doctor to you. If she gets emails or texts from preschool or the youth group leader, contact them and ask them to please contact you instead, or at least in addition to the mom. Put your contact information in the "Parent/Guardian #1" slot on all contact forms for your child.

5. **Find the mom you love three therapists with good ratings, who take her insurance or are otherwise affordable.**

6. **Take care of your physical and mental health.** Mothers do not want the added labor of having to be in charge of your health. *You* be in charge of your health. Your shoulder keeps acting up? See a doctor. You've been feeling sluggish and melancholy for six months? Find an equally good therapist for yourself. You are no good to the mother you love if all your emotions are bottled up inside, and you're not actively working to identify and unlearn the ways the white supremacist capitalist patriarchy has shaped and continues to shape the way you move through the world and your home.

7. **Put the wellness of the partnership on your daily to-do list.** Come up with date ideas. Be the point person for scheduling and finding childcare for them. Find a reputable couples therapist and handle scheduling and payment.

8. **Initiate tackling the latest parenting problem.** Your partner's parenting problem is your parenting problem. If the mom you love is struggling with a parenting issue, offer to just listen and provide empathy. Then bring up that you'd like to look into finding some solutions. Do your research—the internet, the library, other parenting friends. Take the lead on implementing a new approach. By being proactive on parenting issues, you are removing a piece of work from the mom's load and showing her (and the child) that you are an equal partner in the work of child-rearing.

9. **Conduct a reckoning of kid stuff in the house.** Go through the cartons, boxes, drawers, shelves, and closets, and decide which toys and clothes are still useful and which ones should be given away. Coordinate the giving away.

Then figure out what new items are needed (new sneakers for Eva? a hoodie for Malcolm?) and do the work to procure them, whether that's putting out a request to friends with older kids for their hand-me-downs or buying them yourself. Repeat reckoning two to four times annually.

10. **Do a full-day deep clean.** Do a deep tidy, and then a deep clean. The two are separate things. The first involves putting things away, doing and folding laundry, and eliminating clutter. The latter involves a vacuum, a sponge, water, and cleansers. If you have the funds to outsource this work, coordinate, schedule, and handle payment for a housecleaner yourself and figure out how you are going to entertain the children while the house is being cleaned. Educate yourself on domestic worker rates and rights. Repeat monthly.

11. **Give the mom you love a full day off the parenting clock.** (Bonus for scheduling it on the deep-clean day so she returns to a fresh house!) Offer some ideas for how she might like to spend her day. This can be fancy and expensive like a spa day, but with advance notice, it can be low-budget and equally wonderful, like a picnic for her and three of her best friends somewhere beautiful. Double bonus if you set up the day for her by texting with her friends, buying the food, and filling up the picnic basket. Sometimes the work of planning something lovely like a picnic with friends is prohibitively overwhelming for already overworked moms. Having someone plan and coordinate it is almost as good as the day itself. Repeat monthly.

12. **Engage in relationship building.** The work of forming and nurturing social connections falls mostly on mothers, yet all parents directly benefit from this labor. When the mom you love makes friends with another kid's parents,

who then offer to trade off childcare during spring break week, you get two or three days of free childcare thanks to her relational work. Acknowledge the time and energy this work requires, recognize its value, and challenge yourself to begin doing it too. Deliver meals to the parents of a new baby. Bake cookies and deliver them with the kids to a new neighbor. Do school pickups and drop-offs, and engage in the chatting, which is actually relationship building. Invite the neighborhood kids to play a game on the street and be the parent in charge.

13. **Do not contact the mom you love when you are solo parenting.** Don't text her when you are in charge of the kids. Don't ask her where the Tylenol is. She doesn't want to feel bad that you or the kids have a headache. Don't message her *Do you know where Ellie the Elephant is? We can't find her!* You're the parent, not a babysitter. Handle it!

14. **Take on your child's extracurricular activities.** If you and your partner want to put your child in a sport, music lessons, Sunday school, summer camp, or after-school care, tell the mom you love you'll handle it from the *real* start to the *real* finish: research all the options and figure out what your family can afford; troubleshoot how your child will get to and from these activities; contact any of your child's friends who either might want to do the activity, too, or whose parents might have wisdom to share with you; contact and talk to the people who run the activity; relay to your partner all the information and how this new addition to your family's schedule can work. Once you are both in agreement, book and pay for the activity in a timely manner, making sure you list your contact info in the Parent/ Guardian #1 slot, and then enter all the information into your family calendar.

15. **Create flexibility in your work schedule.** Prioritize having a job that gives you the flexibility to leave early or arrive late. Or, if you have racial, economic, heterosexual, or male privilege, use it to advocate for the parenting employees at your job to be given more flexibility for family needs. The entire family dynamic can change if the family's schedule isn't strictly arranged around protecting one parent's work hours. If possible, shift your hours earlier or later on some days so that you can have an equal share (or more) of being in charge of the two most stressful parts of the day: the morning rush and the dinner-to-bedtime slog.

16. **Schedule the appointments and do the chauffeuring during the workday.** Arrange your work hours so you can do school pickups and drop-offs, and schedule and attend your kids' medical appointments. This will force you to be on top of their doctors' names and contact info, and up to date on your kids' health. It'll also ensure that *you* are the parent the teachers and doctors know. After appointments, relay any new information to the mom you love.

17. **Be the point person on vacations (from the *real* start to the *real* finish).** Mothering is decision fatigue. Take some of her fatigue away by researching, scheduling, coordinating, and managing all things vacation, preferably with some built-in childcare.

18. **Demand and take your full family leave.** This is the foundation that will make all of the above happen more naturally. Studies have shown that fathers who take their full paternity leave have a closer relationship with their child in the long term, and their marriages have a more equal division of domestic labor. And, unsurprisingly, based on the first two outcomes, it's been shown that dads who

take their leave are less likely to get divorced. Plus, you'll be setting an example and affecting your company's culture, which has the potential to reduce the mom rage not just in *your* home, but in the homes of coworkers and future employees.

19. **Share something about your parenting that you feel vulnerable about.** Opening up to the mom you love about your struggles can make her feel less alone in parenting. Vulnerability facilitates intimacy. Not for nothing, but partners are way sexier after they open up about their feelings (wink, wink).

Reveal Your Rage Risk Factors

1. **Location.** Are there certain places I tend to rage? The bathroom? The car? On vacation? At the playground?
2. **Other People.** Do I rage only when I'm alone with the kids? The day after I visit my in-laws? After the kids spend time with specific friends?
3. **Times of Day.** What time of day am I raging? Before I've had my morning coffee? Do I rage when the kids are hyper and tired just before dinner? Getting out the door during the morning rush? When the baby won't nap? After school during the homework/screen-time negotiation conversation? Right before bed?
4. **Other Contributing Factors.** When is the last time I ate? How did I sleep the night before? Am I stressed about money? When's the last time I had a couple hours of alone time? When did I last have sex? When's the last time I exercised? Have I been getting enough writing time? Have I been social with my friends?

4 Key Questions to Ask Your Rage

1. Where does it hurt?
2. What are you afraid of?
3. What are you trying to protect?
4. What do you need?

REFERENCES

Prologue

Dubin, Minna. "The Rage Mothers Don't Talk About." *New York Times,* September 13, 2019. www.nytimes.com/2020/04/15/parenting/mother-rage.html.

"How Victorian Women Were Oppressed Through the Use of Psychiatry." *The Atlantic,* November 2017. www.theatlantic.com/sponsored/netflix-2017/how-victorian-women-were-oppressed-through-the-use-of-psychiatry/1607.

Lamott, Anne. "Mother Rage: Theory and Practice." *Salon,* October 29, 1998. www.salon.com/1998/10/29/29lamo_2.

Rich, Adrienne. *Women and Honor: Some Notes on Lying.* Pittsburg: Motheroot Publications, Pittsburgh Women Writers, 1977.

Scarre, Geoffrey, and John Callow. *Witchcraft and Magic in Sixteenth- and Seventeenth-Century Europe.* 2nd ed. Basingstoke, UK: Palgrave Macmillan, 2001.

Solnit, Rebecca. *The Mother of All Questions: Further Feminisms.* Chicago: Haymarket Books, 2017.

Chapter 1

Ellis, Krista. "Race and Poverty Violence in the Child Welfare System: Strategies for Child Welfare Practitioners." *Child Law Practice Today,* December 17, 2019. www.americanbar.org/groups/public_interest/child_law/resources/child_law_practiceonline/january---december-2019/race-and-poverty-bias-in-the-child-welfare-system---strategies-f/.

Guy, Jane. "Mamas, Lockdown, and Me—Minna Dubin." Produced by Jane Guy, *Queenstown Life,* May 12, 2020. Podcast. https://share.transistor.fm/s/057fff71.

Machado, Carmen Maria. *In the Dream House: A Memoir.* Minneapolis, MN: Graywolf Press, 2019.

Montei, Amanda. "I Became a Pandemic 'Wine Mom.' Here's What I Learned." *HuffPost,* August 8, 2021. www.huffpost.com/entry/wine-mom-covid-19-pandemic_n_611bd2f5e4b0ff60bf7a192b.

"Police Violence Map." Mapping Police Violence. Accessed August 30, 2022. https://mappingpoliceviolence.org.

Chapter 2

Anderson, Julie. "Breadwinner Mothers by Race/Ethnicity and State." *Institute for Women's Policy Research Quick Figures*, September 2016. https://iwpr.org/wp-content/uploads/2020/08/Q054.pdf.

"Average Amount Millennial Parents Spend on Parenting Books and Apps in This Field?" Wonder, August 7, 2017. https://askwonder.com/research/avg-amount-millennial-parents-spend-parenting-books-apps-field-great-break-down-xjjsxbcdl.

Becker, Sascha O., Anna Fernandes, and Doris Weichselbaumer. "Discrimination in Hiring Based on Potential and Realized Fertility: Evidence from a Large-Scale Field Experiment." *Labour Economics* 59 (2019): 139–152. https://doi.org/10.24451/arbor.12320.

Biss, Eula. "Of Institution Born," foreword to *Of Woman Born: Motherhood as Experience and Institution*, by Adrienne Rich, xiv–xvii. New York: W. W. Norton & Company, Inc., 2021.

Calhoun, Ada. "The New Midlife Crisis: Why (and How) It's Hitting Gen X Women." *O, the Oprah Magazine*, October 9, 2017. www.oprah.com/sp/new-midlife-crisis.html.

Chua, Amy. *The Battle Hymn of the Tiger Mother.* New York: Penguin Books, 2011.

Ciciolla, Lucia, and Suniya S. Luthar. "Invisible Household Labor and Ramifications for Adjustment: Mothers as Captains of Households." *Sex Roles* 81 (October 2019): 467–486. https://doi.org/10.1007/s11199-018-1001-x.

Coontz, Stephanie. "How to Make Your Marriage Gayer." *New York Times*, February 13, 2020. www.nytimes.com/2020/02/13/opinion/sunday/marriage-housework-gender-happiness.html.

Cyca, Michelle. "Instagram's Parent Trap." *The Walrus*, October 19, 2021. https://thewalrus.ca/instagrams-parent-trap.

Druckerman, Pamela. *Bringing Up Bébé: One American Mother Discovers the Wisdom of French Parenting.* New York: Penguin Books, 2014.

Hays, Sharon. *The Cultural Contradictions of Motherhood.* New Haven: Yale University Press, 1996.

Jha, Manish K., Maurizio Fava, Abu Minhajuddin, Cherise Chin Fatt, David Mischoulon, Nausheen Wakhlu, et al. "Anger Attacks Are Associated with Persistently Elevated Irritability in MDD: Findings from the EMBARC Study." *Psychological Medicine* 51, no. 8 (2021): 1355–1363. https://doi.org/10.1017/S0033291720000112.

Livingston, Gretchen. *Growing Number of Dads Home with the Kids.* Washington, DC: PEW Research Center, June 5, 2014. www.pewresearch.org/social-trends/2014/06/05/growing-number-of-dads-home-with-the-kids/.

Livingston, Gretchen. "Stay-at-Home Moms and Dads Account for About One-in-Five US Parents." PEW Research Center, September 24, 2018. www.pewresearch.org/fact-tank/2018/09/24/stay-at-home-moms-and-dads-account-for-about-one-in-five-u-s-parents.

Lorde, Audre. "The Uses of Anger: Women Responding to Racism." Keynote address at the National Women's Studies Association Convention, June 1981. Transcript. https://academicworks.cuny.edu/cgi/viewcontent.cgi?article=1654&context=wsq.

Miller, Claire Cain. "How Same-Sex Couples Divide Chores and What It Reveals About Modern Parenting." *New York Times*, May 16, 2018. www.nytimes.com/2018/05/16/upshot/same-sex-couples-divide-chores-much-more-evenly-until-they-become-parents.html.

O'Reilly, Andrea. "Teaching Motherhood Studies: From Normative Motherhood to Empowered Mothering." Paper presented at the MIRCI twentieth anniversary conference in Toronto, October 2016. www.academia.edu/30059596/TEACHING_MOTHERHOOD_STUDIES_From_Normative_Motherhood_to_Empowered_Mothering.

PEW Research Center. "The Harried Life of the Working Mother." PEW Research Center, October 1, 2009. www.pewresearch.org/social-trends/2009/10/01/the-harried-life-of-the-working-mother.

Remes, Olivia, Carol Brayne, Rianne van der Linde, and Louise Lafortune. "A Systematic Review of Reviews on the Prevalence of Anxiety Disorders in Adult Populations." *Brain and Behavior* 6, no. 7 (June 5, 2016). https://doi.org/10.1002/brb3.497.

Rich, Adrienne. *Of Woman Born: Motherhood as Experience and Institution*. New York: W. W. Norton & Company, Inc., 1995.

Romolini, Jennifer. "Calm Down," episode 93. Produced by Jennifer Romolini and Kim France, *Everything Is Fine*, March 14, 2022. Podcast.

Scharrer, Erica, Stephen Warren, Eean Grimshaw, Gichuhi Kamau, Sarah Cho, Menno Reijven, and Congcong Zhang. "Disparaged Dads? A Content Analysis of Depictions of Fathers in US Sitcoms Over Time." *Psychology of Popular Media* 10, no. 2 (2021): 275–287. https://doi.org/10.1037/ppm0000289.

Shrider, Emily A., Melissa Kollar, Frances Chen, and Jessica Semega. *Income and Poverty in the United States: 2020*. Washington, DC: United States Census Bureau, September 14, 2021. www.census.gov/library/publications/2021/demo/p60-273.html.

Stankorb, Sarah. "Glad to Be a Xennial." *Good Magazine*, September 25, 2014. www.good.is/articles/generation-xennials.

Takseva, Tatjana. "How Contemporary Consumerism Shapes Intensive Mothering." In *Intensive Mothering: The Cultural Contradictions of Modern Motherhood*, edited by Linda Rose Ennis, 211–232. Ontario: Demeter Press, 2014.

Tucker, Jasmine. *Equal Pay for Mothers Is Critical for Families*. Washington, DC: National Women's Law Center, June 2019. https://nwlc.org/wp-content/uploads/2019/06/Moms-EPD-v5.pdf.

United States Bureau of Labor and Statistics. "Household Data Annual Averages: Employed and Unemployed Full- and Part-Time Workers by Age, Sex, Race, and Hispanic or Latino Ethnicity." Current Population Survey, 2021. www.bls.gov/cps/cpsaat08.htm.

United States Census Bureau. "Table PINC-05: Work Experience-People Fifteen Years Old and Over, by Total Money Earnings, Age, Race, Hispanic Origin, Sex, and Disability Status." Current Population Survey (CPS) Annual Social and Economic (ASEC) Supplement. Last modified October 8, 2021. www.census.gov/data/tables/time-series/demo/income-poverty/cps-pinc/pinc-05.html.

United States Department of Labor. "Employment Characteristics of Families—2020." News release no. USDL-22-0673, April 21, 2021. www.bls.gov/news.release/pdf/famee.pdf.

West, Mary (Mrs. Max). *Infant Care*. US Department of Labor Children's Bureau Pub. Issues 1–9, 59–60. Washington: Government Printing Office, 1914. www.mchlibrary.org/history/chbu/3121-1914.PDF.

"Working Fathers Get 21% 'Wage Bonus,' TUC Study Suggests." British Broadcasting Corporation, April 25, 2016. www.bbc.com/news/business-36126584.

Chapter 3

Angel, Sherry. "Scientific Dream Team Aims to Make Preeclampsia a Relic of the Past." Cedars Sinai, July 1, 2019. www.cedars-sinai.org/discoveries/2019/a-race-against-lightning.html.

Biden, Joseph. State of the Union Address, March 1, 2022. Transcript. www.whitehouse.gov/state-of-the-union-2022.

Brown, Hilary K. "Disparities in Severe Maternal Morbidity and Mortality—A Call for Inclusion of Disability in Obstetric Research and Health Care Professional Education." *Obstetrics and Gynecology* 4, no. 12 (2021). https://doi.org/10.1001/jamanetworkopen.2021.38910.

The Century Foundation. "Closing America's Education Funding Gaps." The Century Foundation, July 22, 2020. https://tcf.org/content/report/closing-americas-education-funding.

Chzhen, Yekaterina, Anna Gromada, and Gwyther Rees. *Are the World's Richest Countries Family Friendly? Policy in the OECD and EU*. Florence: UNICEF Office of Research, June 2019. www.unicef-irc.org/family-friendly.

Cooper, Brittney. *Eloquent Rage: A Black Feminist Discovers Her Superpower*. New York: Picador, 2018.

Dell'Antonia, KJ. "The Families That Can't Afford Summer." *New York Times*, June 4, 2016. www.nytimes.com/2016/06/05/sunday-review/the-families-that-cant-afford-summer.html.

DeSilver, Drew. "For Most US Workers, Real Wages Have Barely Budged in Decades." PEW Research Center, August 7, 2018. www.pewresearch.org/fact-tank/2018/08/07/for-most-us-workers-real-wages-have-barely-budged-for-decades.

Diament, Michelle. "Autism Moms Have Stress Similar to Combat Soldiers." Disability Scoop, November 10, 2009. www.disabilityscoop.com/2009/11/10/autism-moms-stress/6121/.

Diamond, Rachel M., Kristina S. Brown, and Jennifer Miranda. "Impact of COVID-19 on the Perinatal Period Through a Biopsychosocial Systemic Framework." *Contemporary Family Therapy* 42, no. 3 (2020): 205–216. https://doi.org/10.1007/s10591-020-09544-8.

Domar, Alice D., Patricia C. Zuttermeister, and Richard Friedman. "The Psychological Impact of Infertility: A Comparison with Patients with Other Medical Conditions." *Journal of Psychosomatic Obstetrics and Gynecology* 14 (1993): 45–52. https://pubmed.ncbi.nlm.nih.gov/8142988/.

Fabian-Weber, Nicole. "Summer Camp Cost: Breaking Down the Price of Day, Sleep-Away, and Specialty Camps." Care.com, March 16, 2022. www.care.com/c /what-does-summer-camp-cost.

Herman, Juliana, et al. "The United States Is Far Behind Other Countries on Pre-K." Center for American Progress, May 2, 2013. www.americanprogress.org/article /the-united-states-is-far-behind-other-countries-on-pre-k.

"Higher Education for Foster Youth." National Youth Foster Institute, accessed November 20, 2022. https://nfyi.org/issues/higher-education.

Kamenetz, Anya. "Parents and Caregivers of Young Children Say They've Hit Pandemic Rock Bottom." NPR, January 20, 2022. www.npr.org/2022/01/20/1074182352 /unvaccinated-young-kids-child-care-parents-omicron-disruptions.

Liu, Cindy H., Carmina Erdei, and Leena Mittal. "Risk Factors for Depression, Anxiety, and PTSD Symptoms in Perinatal Women During the COVID-19 Pandemic." *Psychiatry Research* 295 (January 2021). https://doi.org/10 .1016/j.psychres.2020.113552.

Maciesz, Patti. Bill the Patriarchy. Website. www.billthepatriarchy.com.

Madowitz, Michael, Alex Rowell, and Katie Hamm. *Calculating the Hidden Cost of Interrupting a Career for Child Care*. Washington, DC: Center for American Progress, June 2016. www.americanprogress.org/wp-content/uploads/2016/06 /ChildCareCalculator-methodology.pdf.

Miller, Claire Cain. "How Other Nations Pay for Child Care. The US Is an Outlier." *New York Times*, October 6, 2021. www.nytimes.com/2021/10/06/upshot /child-care-biden.html.

National Domestic Workers Alliance. Website, accessed October 31, 2022. www .domesticworkers.org/about-domestic-work.

Oxfam International. "Not All Gaps Are Created Equal: The True Value of Care Work." Oxfam International. www.oxfam.org/en/not-all-gaps-are -created-equal-true-value-care-work.

Parker, Kim. "Women More Than Men Adjust Their Careers for Family Life." PEW Research Center, October 1, 2015. www.pewresearch.org/fact-tank/2015/10/01 /women-more-than-men-adjust-their-careers-for-family-life.

Petersen, Anne Helen. "The Past and Potential Future of the Summer Care Scramble." *Culture Study*, March 20, 2022. https://annehelen.substack.com/p /the-past-and-potential-future-of.

Petts, Richard J., Chris Knoester, and Qi Li. "Paid Paternity Leave-Taking in the United States." *Community, Work and Family* 23, no. 2 (2020): 162–183. https://doi .org/10.1080/13668803.2018.1471589.

PEW Research Center. "Balancing Work and Family." *On Pay Gap, Millennial Women Near Parity—for Now*. Washington, DC: PEW Research Center, December 11, 2013. www.pewresearch.org/social-trends/2013/12/11/chapter -5-balancing-work-and-family.

Precedence Research. "Fertility Market Size, Share, Trends, Growth Report 2021–2027." Ontario, Canada: Precedence Research, accessed November 20, 2022. www.precedenceresearch.com/fertility-market.

Rabin, Roni Caryn. "Huge Racial Disparities Found in Deaths Linked to Pregnancy." *New York Times*, May 7, 2019. www.nytimes.com/2019/05/07/health/pregnancy-deaths-.html.

Redford, Jeremy, and Stephanie Burns. *The Summer After Kindergarten: Children's Experiences by Socioeconomic Characteristics*. Washington, DC: US Department of Education National Center for Education Statistics, May 2018. https://nces.ed.gov/pubs2018/2018160.pdf.

Rooney, Kristin L., and Alice D. Domar. "The Relationship Between Stress and Infertility." *Dialogues in Clinical Neuroscience* 20, no. 1 (2018): 41–47. https://doi.org/10.31887/DCNS.2018.20.1/klrooney.

Salam, Maya. "'Vagina Obscura' Demystifies Female Anatomy." Review of *Vagina Obscura* by Rachel E. Gross. *New York Times*, March 9, 2022. www.nytimes.com/2022/03/29/books/vagina-obscura-rachel-gross.html.

Smith, Leann E., Jan S. Greenberg, and Marsha Mailick Seltzer. "Social Support and Well-Being at Mid-Life Among Mothers of Adolescents and Adults with Autism Spectrum Disorders." *Journal of Autism and Developmental Disorders* 42 (2012): 1818–1826. https://doi.org/10.1007/s10803-011-1420-9.

Smith, Leann E., Jinkuk Hong, Marsha Mailick Seltzer, Jan S. Greenberg, David M. Almeida, and Somer L. Bishop. "Daily Experiences Among Mothers of Adolescents and Adults with Autism Spectrum Disorder." *Journal of Autism and Developmental Disorders* 40 (2010): 167–178. https://doi.org/10.1007/s10803-009-0844-y.

Tecco, Halle, and Julia Cheek. "Women's Health Is More Than Female Anatomy and Our Reproductive System—It's About Unraveling Centuries of Inequities Due to Living in a Patriarchal Healthcare System." *Harvard Business School Health Care Blog*, January 18, 2022. www.hbs.edu/healthcare/blog/post/defining-womens-health-womens-health-is-more-than-female-anatomy-and-our-reproductive-systemits-about-unraveling-centuries-of-inequities-due-to-living-in-a-patriarchal-healthcare-system.

Thier, Jane. "The Cost of Childcare Has Risen by 41% During the Pandemic with Families Spending Up to 20% of Their Salaries." *Fortune*, January 28, 2022. https://fortune.com/2022/01/28/the-cost-of-child-care-in-the-us-is-rising.

Tikkanen, Roosa, Munira Z. Gunja, Molly FitzGerald, and Laurie Zephyrin. "Maternal Mortality and Maternity Care in the United States Compared to Ten Other Developed Countries." The Commonwealth Fund, November 18, 2020. www.commonwealthfund.org/publications/issue-briefs/2020/nov/maternal-mortality-maternity-care-us-compared-10-countries.

United States Centers for Medicare and Medicaid Services. "Who Enrolls in Medicaid and CHIP?" Medicaid.gov, accessed June 27, 2022. www.medicaid.gov/state-overviews/scorecard/who-enrolls-medicaid-chip/index.html.

United States Department of Health and Human Services Office of the Secretary. "2021 Poverty Guidelines." February 1, 2021. www.govinfo.gov/content/pkg/FR-2021-02-01/pdf/2021-01969.pdf.

United States Department of Labor. "Unpaid Eldercare in the United States—2017-2018 Summary." News release no. USDL-19-2051, November 22, 2019. www.bls.gov/news.release/elcare.nr0.htm.

United States Department of Labor. "Occupational Employment and Wages, May 2021: Childcare Workers." US Bureau of Labor Statistics, May 2021. https://stats.bls.gov/oes/current/oes399011.htm.

United States Department of Labor. "Labor Force Statistics from the Current Population Survey." US Bureau of Labor Statistics, 2021. www.bls.gov/cps/cpsaat11.htm.

United States Health Resources and Services Administration. "Children with Special Health Care Needs." National Survey of Children's Health Data Brief, July 2020. https://mchb.hrsa.gov/sites/default/files/mchb/programs-impact/nsch-cshcn-data-brief.pdf.

Williams, David R. "Stress and the Mental Health of Populations of Color: Advancing Our Understanding of Race-Related Stressors." *Journal of Health and Social Behavior* 59, no. 4 (2018): 466–485. https://doi.org/10.1177/0022146518814251.

Chapter 4

Athan, Aurélie. Matrescence. Website. www.matrescence.com.

Athan, Aurélie. "Matrescence: The Emerging Mother." Medium, March 8, 2019. https://medium.com/@ama81/matrescence-the-emerging-mother-69d1699ff0cc.

Athan, Aurélie, and Heather L. Reel. "Maternal Psychology: Reflections on the Twentieth Anniversary of *Deconstructing Developmental Psychology*." *Feminism and Psychology* 25, no. 3 (August 2015): 311–325. https://doi.org/10.1177/0959353514562804.

Carmona, Susanna. "Matrescence and Adolescence: Which Has a Greater Impact on the Brain?" Produced by Jodi Pawluski, *Mommy Brain Revisited*, June 5, 2020. Podcast. www.jodipawluski.com/mommybrainrevisited/episode/255940bc/6-matrescence-and-adolescence-which-has-a-greater-impact-on-the-brain.

Carmona, Susanna, Magdalena Martínez-Garcia, Maria Paternina-Die, Erika Barba-Müller, Lara M. Wierenga, Yasser Alemán-Gómez, et al. "Pregnancy and Adolescence Entail Similar Neuroanatomical Adaptations: A Comparative Analysis of Cerebral Morphometric Changes." *Human Brain Mapping* 40, no. 7 (2019): 2143–2152. https://doi.org/10.1002/hbm.24513.

Hoekzema, Elseline, Erika Barba-Müller, Cristina Pozzobon, Marisol Picado, Florencio Lucco, David García-García, Juan Carlos Soliva, et al. "Pregnancy Leads to Long-Lasting Changes in Human Brain Structure." *Nature Neuroscience* 20. (2017): 287–296. https://doi.org/10.1038/nn.4458.

hooks, bell. *Communion: The Female Search for Love*. New York: William Morrow, 2002.

King, Ruth. *Healing Rage: Women Making Inner Peace Possible*. New York: Gotham Books, 2007.

PEW Research Center. "How Mothers and Fathers Spend Their Time." *Modern Parenthood: Roles of Moms and Dads Converge as They Balance Work and Family*. Washington, DC: PEW Research Center, March 14, 2013. www.pewresearch.org/social-trends/2013/03/14/chapter-4-how-mothers-and-fathers-spend-their-time.

Sacks, Alexandra. "The Birth of a Mother." *New York Times*, May 8, 2017. www.nytimes.com/2017/05/08/well/family/the-birth-of-a-mother.html.

Sacks, Alexandra. "Matrescence: The Developmental Transition to Motherhood." *Psychology Today*, April 8, 2019. www.psychologytoday.com/us/blog/motherhood -unfiltered/201904/matrescence-the-developmental-transition-motherhood.

Swarns, Rachel L. "When Their Workday Ends, More Fathers Are Heading into the Kitchen." *New York Times*, November 23, 2014. www.nytimes.com/2014/11/24/ nyregion/when-the-workday-ends-more-fathers-are-heading-to-the-kitchen.html.

Tasca, Cecilia, Mariangela Rapetti, Mauro Giovanni Carta, and Bianca Fadda. "Women and Hysteria in the History of Mental Health." *Clinical Practice and Epidemiology in Mental Health* 8 (2012): 110–119. https://doi.org/10.2174/17450179012 08010110.

Yoder, Rachel. *Nightbitch*. New York: Doubleday, 2021.

Zimmerman, Erin. "The Identity Transformation of Becoming a Mom." *The Cut*, May 25, 2018. www.thecut.com/2018/05/the-identity-transformation-of -becoming-a-mom.html.

Chapter 5

Benson, Kyle. "The Magic Relationship Ratio, According to Science." The Gottman Institute, accessed November 20, 2022. www.gottman.com/blog /the-magic-relationship-ratio-according-science.

Brescoll, Victoria L., and Eric Luis Uhlmann. "Can an Angry Woman Get Ahead? Status Conferral, Gender, and Expression of Emotion in the Workplace." *Psychological Science* 19, no. 3 (2008): 268–275. https://doi.org/10.1111/j.1467-9280.2008.02079.x.

Brown, Brené. "The Gift of Imperfect Parenting—with Brené Brown," Session 1. Produced by Tami Simon, *Sounds True*, November 30, 2014. Podcast. https:// resources.soundstrue.com/blog/gifts-imperfect-parenting-brene-brown.

Burgard, Sarah A. "The Needs of Others: Gender and Sleep Interruptions for Caregivers." *Social Forces* 89, no. 4 (June 2011): 1189–1215. https://doi.org/10.1093/sf /89.4.1189.

Carey, Benedict. "Evidence That Little Touches Do Mean So Much." *New York Times*, February 22, 2010. www.nytimes.com/2010/02/23/health/23mind.html.

Goleman, Daniel. *Emotional Intelligence: Why It Can Matter More Than IQ*. New York: Bantam Books, 1995.

Jamison, Leslie. "I Used to Insist I Didn't Get Angry. Not Anymore." *New York Times Magazine*, January 17, 2018. www.nytimes.com/2018/01/17/magazine/i-used -to-insist-i-didnt-get-angry-not-anymore.html.

Krizan, Zlatan, and Garrett Hisler. "Sleepy Anger: Restricted Sleep Amplifies Angry Feelings." *Journal of Experimental Psychology: General* 148, no. 7 (2019): 1239–1250. https://doi.org/10.1037/xge0000522.

Min, Sung Kil, Shin-Young Suh, and Ki-Jun Song. "Symptoms to Use for Diagnostic Criteria of Hwa-Byung, an Anger Syndrome." *Psychiatry Investigation* 6, no. 1 (2009): 7–12. https://doi.org/10.4306/pi.2009.6.1.7.

Ou, Christine H. K., and Wendy A. Hall. "Anger in the Context of Postnatal Depression: An Integrative Review." *Birth* 45, no. 4 (2018): 343. https://doi.org/10.1111 /birt.12356.

Ou, Christine H. K., Wendy A. Hall, Paddy Rodney, and Robyn Stremler. "Correlates of Canadian Mothers' Anger During the Postpartum Period: A Cross-Sectional

Survey." *BMC Pregnancy and Childbirth* 22, no. 163 (2022). https://doi.org/10.1186 /s12884-022-04479-4.

Rebhun, Linda-Anne. "Swallowing Frogs: Anger and Illness in Northeast Brazil." *Medical Anthropology Quarterly* 8, no. 4 (1994): 360–382. https://doi.org/10.1525 /maq.1994.8.4.02a00030.

Sturge-Apple, Melissa L., Michael A. Skibo, Fred A. Rogosch, Zeljko Ignjatovic, and Wendi Heinzelman. "The Impact of Allostatic Load on Maternal Sympathovagal Functioning in Stressful Child Contexts: Implications for Problematic Parenting." *Development and Psychopathology* 23, no. 3 (2011): 831–844. https://doi.org/10.1017 /S0954579411000332.

Yao, Diamond. "The Revolutionary Anger of Asian Women." Autostraddle, June 10, 2021. www.autostraddle.com/the-revolutionary-anger-of-asian-women.

Chapter 6

Chemaly, Soraya. "Why Women Don't Get to Be Angry." *Medium*, September 18, 2018. https://gen.medium.com/rage-becomes-her-why-women-dont-get-to-be -angry-b2496e9d679d.

Fields, R. Douglas. *Why We Snap: Understanding the Rage Circuit in Your Brain.* New York: Dutton, 2016.

Lorde, Audre. "The Uses of Anger: Women Responding to Racism." Keynote address at the National Women's Studies Association Convention, June 1981. Transcript. https://academicworks.cuny.edu/cgi/viewcontent.cgi?article=1654&context=wsq.

Okun, Tema. "White Supremacy Culture." Dismantling Racism (dRWORKS), n.d. https://dismantlingracism.org/uploads/4/3/5/7/43579015/okun_-_white _sup_culture.pdf.

Olff, Miranda. "Sex and Gender Differences in Post-Traumatic Stress Disorder: An Update." *European Journal of Psychotraumatology* 8, no. 4 (2017). https://doi.org/10.10 80/20008198.2017.1351204.

Ou, Christine H. K., and Wendy A. Hall. "Anger in the Context of Postnatal Depression: An Integrative Review." *Birth* 45, no. 4 (2018): 343. https://doi.org/10.1111 /birt.12356.

Pilon, Mary. "Monopoly's Inventor: The Progressive Who Didn't Pass 'Go.'" *New York Times*, February 13, 2015. www.nytimes.com/2015/02/15/business /behind-monopoly-an-inventor-who-didnt-pass-go.html.

Powell, Alvin. "When Science Meets Mindfulness." *The Harvard Gazette*, April 9, 2018. https://news.harvard.edu/gazette/story/2018/04/harvard-researchers-study -how-mindfulness-may-change-the-brain-in-depressed-patients.

Sweeton, Jennifer. "To Heal Trauma, Work with the Body." *Psychology Today*, August 20, 2017. www.psychologytoday.com/us/blog/workings-well-being/201708 /heal-trauma-work-the-body.

Treace, Bonnie Myotai. "Rising to the Challenge: Filling the Well with Snow." *Tricycle: The Buddhist Review*, Spring 2003. https://tricycle.org/magazine/rising-challenge -filling-well-snow.

Vernor, Dale. "PTSD Is More Likely in Women Than Men." *NAMI Blog.* National Alliance on Mental Illness, October 8, 2019. www.nami.org/Blogs/NAMI-Blog /October-2019/PTSD-is-More-Likely-in-Women-Than-Men.

Chapter 7

Brescoll, Victoria L., and Eric Luis Uhlmann. "Can an Angry Woman Get Ahead? Status Conferral, Gender, and Expression of Emotion in the Workplace." *Psychological Science* 19, no. 3 (2008): 268–275. https://doi.org/10.1111/j.1467-9280.2008.02079.x.

Krauss, Nicole. *The History of Love.* New York: W. W. Norton & Company, Inc., 2005.

Kring, Ann M., and Albert H. Gordon. "Sex Differences in Emotion: Expression, Experience, and Physiology." *Journal of Personality and Social Psychology* 74, no. 3 (1998): 686–703. https://doi.org/10.1037/0022-3514.74.3.686.

Potter-Efron, Ronald T. *Rage: A Step-by-Step Guide to Overcoming Explosive Anger.* Oakland: New Harbinger Publications, 2007.

The Zones of Regulation. Website. www.zonesofregulation.com.

Chapter 8

Avendano, Mauricio, Lisa F. Berkman, Agar Brugiavin, and Giacomo Pasin. "The Long-Run Effect of Maternity Leave Benefits on Mental Health: Evidence from European Countries." *Social Science & Medicine* 132 (2015): 45–53. https://doi.org/10.1016/j.socscimed.2015.02.037.

Brewer, Kristie. "The Day Iceland's Women Went on Strike." BBC, October 23, 2015. www.bbc.com/news/magazine-34602822.

Buck, Stephanie. "Iceland Came to a Halt When 90% of Women Walked Off the Job in the 1970s." *Business Insider*, March 12, 2017. www.businessinsider.com/iceland-came-to-a-halt-when-90-of-women-walked-off-the-job-in-the-70s-2017-3.

"Childcare Center Opened by Mayor." *New York Times*, January 26, 1943. https://timesmachine.nytimes.com/timesmachine/1943/01/26/87408284.html?pageNumber=16.

Einarsdóttir, Halla Kristín, dir. *Women in Red Stockings*. 2009. Reykjavík: The Icelandic Oral History Center, 2015. Video. https://vimeo.com/141731463.

"Equality Maps: Family Leave Laws." Movement Advancement Project, accessed June 27, 2022. www.lgbtmap.org/equality-maps/fmla_laws.

Garbes, Angela. *Essential Labor: Mothering as Social Change.* New York: Harper Wave, 2022.

Gil, Natalie. "Why Women in Iceland Walked Out of Work at 2:38 P.M. Today." *Refinery29*, October 24, 2016. www.refinery29.com/en-gb/2016/10/127356/iceland-women-gender-pay-gay-protest-leaving-work-early.

Gilligan, Carol. *In a Different Voice: Psychological Theory and Women's Development.* Cambridge, MA: Harvard University Press, 1982.

Gilligan, Carol. "Carol Gilligan." Interview by Ethics of Care, June 21, 2011. https://ethicsofcare.org/carol-gilligan.

hooks, bell. *Feminist Theory: From Margin to Center.* Cambridge, MA: South End Press, 1984.

Kiesling, Lydia. "Paid Child Care for Mothers? All It Took Was a World War." *New York Times*, October 2, 2019. www.nytimes.com/2019/10/02/us/paid-childcare-working-mothers-wwii.html.

Lawyers Committee for Civil Rights Under Law. *Paid Family Leave—Racial Justice Implications*. Lawyers Committee for Civil Rights Under Law, June 2019. https://lawyerscommittee.org/wp-content/uploads/2019/06/2019-6-5-Paid -Leave-Racial-Justice-Fact-Sheet-Final.pdf.

Parolin, Zachary, Sophie Collyera, Megan A. Currana, and Christopher Wimera. "Monthly Poverty Rates Among Children After the Expansion of the Child Tax Credit." *Poverty and Social Policy Brief* 5, no. 4 (August 20, 2021). https:// static1.squarespace.com/static/610831a16c95260dbd68934a/t/6125831bb2d0c b07e98375b9/1629848348974/Monthly-Poverty-with-CTC-July-CPSP-2021.pdf.

Persson, Petra, and Maya Rossin-Slater. "When Dad Can Stay Home: Fathers' Workplace Flexibility and Maternal Health." NBER Working Paper Series 25902, National Bureau of Economic Research, Cambridge, MA, May 2019. https://doi .org/10.3386/w25902.

Petts, Richard J., Daniel L. Carlson, and Chris Knoester. "If I [Take] Leave, Will You Stay? Paternity Leave and Relationship Stability." *Journal of Social Policy* 49, no. 4 (2020): 829–849. https://doi.org/10.1017/S0047279419000928.

Schaefer, Louisa. "Something's Amiss, Mom!" *DW*, September 5, 2011. www.dw.com /en/mother-child-health-retreats-give-frazzled-moms-a-boost/a-15355294.

Stevenson, Betsey. "An 'Experiment' in Universal Child Care in the United States: Lessons from the Lanham Act." The Obama White House Archives, January 22, 2015. https://obamawhitehouse.archives.gov/blog/2015/01/22 /experiment-universal-child-care-united-states-lessons-lanham-act.

Stoltzfus, Emilie. *Child Care: The Federal Role During World War II*. Washington, DC: Congressional Research Service, June 29, 2001. https://crsreports.congress.gov /product/pdf/RS/RS20615/9.

Tronto, Joan C. "The Challenges of Medical Care in a Caring Democracy." Presentation at the Plateforme interdisciplinaire d'éthique de l'Université de Lausanne, Lausanne, Switzerland, June 7, 2013. Video, 4:59. www.youtube.com /watch?v=91g5IvWDhqk&t=44s.

Chapter 9

Birdsong, Mia. *How We Show Up: Reclaiming Family, Friendship, and Community*. New York: Hachette Books, 2020.

brown, adrienne maree. *Emergent Strategy: Shaping Change, Changing Worlds*. Chico, CA: AK Press, 2017.

Cohn, D'Vera, Juliana Menasce Horowitz, Rachel Minkin, Richard Fry, and Kiley Hurst. *Financial Issues Top the List of Reasons US Adults Live in Multigenerational Homes*. Washington, DC: PEW Research Center, March 24, 2022. www.pew research.org/social-trends/2022/03/24/financial-issues-top-the-list-of-reasons-u -s-adults-live-in-multigenerational-homes.

Collins, Patricia Hill. *Black Feminist Thought: Knowledge, Consciousness, and the Politics of Empowerment*. New York: Routledge, 1990.

Gawlik, Kate, and Bernadette Mazurek Melnyk. *Pandemic Parenting: Examining the Epidemic of Working Parental Burnout and Strategies to Help*. The Ohio State University, Office of the Chief of Wellness Officer and College of Nursing, May 2022. https://

wellness.osu.edu/sites/default/files/documents/2022/05/OCWO_ParentalBurn-out_3674200_Report_FINAL.pdf.

Gurin, Gerald, Joseph Veroff, and Sheila Feld. "Americans View Their Mental Health, 1957." Inter-University Consortium for Political and Social Research [distributor] (February 16, 1992). https://doi.org/10.3886/ICPSR03503.v1.

Hrdy, Sarah Blaffer. "Mothers and Others." *Natural History* 110, no. 4 (May 2001): 50–63. www.naturalhistorymag.com/picks-from-the-past/11440 /mothers-and-others.

Lakshmin, Pooja. "How Society Has Turned Its Back on Mothers." *New York Times*, February 4, 2021. www.nytimes.com/2021/02/04/parenting/working-mom -burnout-coronavirus.html.

Mead, Margaret. *Coming of Age in Samoa: A Psychological Study of Primitive Youth for Western Civilisation.* New York: Morrow Quill, 1961.

Moors, Amy C., Amanda N. Gesselman, and Justin R. Garcia. "Desire, Familiar-ity, and Engagement in Polyamory: Results from a National Sample of Single Adults in the United States." *Frontiers in Psychology* (March 23, 2021). https://doi .org/10.3389/fpsyg.2021.619640.

National Association of Child Care Resource and Referral Agencies. *Grandpar-ents: A Critical Child Care Safety Net.* National Association of Child Care Re-source and Referral Agencies, 2008. www.childcareaware.org/wp-content /uploads/2015/10/2008_grandparents_report-finalrept.pdf.

O'Reilly, Andrea. "Teaching Motherhood Studies: From Normative Mother-hood to Empowered Mothering." Paper presented at the MIRCI twentieth an-niversary conference in Toronto, October 2016. www.academia.edu/30059596 /TEACHING_MOTHERHOOD_STUDIES_From_Normative_Motherhood _to_Empowered_Mothering.

Palmer, Amanda. *The Art of Asking: Or How I Learned to Stop Worrying and Let People Help.* New York: Grand Central Publishing, 2015.

PEW Research Center. *Parenting in America: Outlook, Worries, Aspirations Are Strongly Linked to Financial Situation.* Washington, DC: PEW Research Cen-ter, December 17, 2015. www.pewresearch.org/social-trends/2015/12/17/1-the -american-family-today.

Rubin, Jennifer D., Amy C. Moors, Jes L. Matsick, Ali Ziegler, and Terri D. Conley. "On the Margins: Considering Diversity Among Consensually Non-Monogamous Relationships." *Journal für Psychologie* 22, no. 1 (2014): 19–37. https://digital commons.chapman.edu/psychology_articles/133/.

"Samoan Baby and Baby-Tender [Anthropology Text]." Item 366 from Children and Youth in History. Accessed November 1, 2022. https://chnm.gmu.edu/cyh /primary-sources/366.html.

Simpo, Ashley. "For Black Women, There's More Than One Way to Be a 'Mother.'" *Par-ents*, March 1, 2022. www.parents.com/kindred/the-legacy-of-black-motherhood -is-expansive-and-cooperative.

INDEX

Credit: Morgan Shidler Photography

Minna Dubin (she/her) is a writer and mother in the San Francisco Bay Area. Her writing has appeared in the *New York Times, Salon, Parents, Philadelphia Inquirer, Romper, Forward, Hobart, MUTHA Magazine,* and *Literary Mama*. She is the recipient of an artist enrichment grant from the Kentucky Foundation for Women. As a leading feminist voice on mom rage, Minna has appeared on MSNBC, *Good Morning America, The Tamron Hall Show,* NBC10 Boston, and NPR.

Website: www.minnadubin.com

Instagram: @minnadubin